CW00590516

The RETRO COOKBOOK

Contents

Then & NOW

In a culinary sense we've come a long way in the last 50 years or so, but we still love the food from the fifties and sixties. It's now affectionately called comfort or retro food. Pamela Clark, Food Director of The Australian Women's Weekly Test Kitchen has 'been there, done that'. Here's her take on Then & Now.

Retro food is back in a big way, everybody's cooking it, talking about it and eating it – in restaurants, at home, at pubs, cafés and bistros.

It was good hearty, flavoursome food. Recipes were short as there weren't too many exotic ingredients to choose from and the basics were put together in myriad ways with huge success. Meals were planned ahead, most home cooks had a repertoire of about 12 recipes, so they were simply rotated. Almost every family had a roast for Sunday lunch, a day when families traditionally got together for a meal. Then there was cold meat left over for sandwiches the next day – not to mention bubble and squeak made from leftover vegies for breakfast on Monday morning – yum!

Most of the cooking for the family was done by the woman of the house – it was her job, along with looking after the house and children, and it was rare for these jobs to be shared with the man of the house. And, who could forget the complicated formal dinner parties of yesteryear – guess who cooked for those – mostly the women of course. It was unusual for men to cook at home, either for the family, or for dinner parties – how times have changed.

Today, most adults work. As a result, household jobs – including the cooking – are shared. There was a time when the superwomen of the fifties and sixties tried to do it all, as they made the transition from home to the workforce. That was never going to work out well for anyone. People are now more food- and health-savvy than ever before; we have never had such easy access to such a wide variety of good-quality ingredients. Food that was considered exotic or that had to be sourced from far away suburbs or specialty shops, even 10 years ago, can now almost certainly be found in supermarkets. Then there are the many growers' markets popping up everywhere – these are a wonderful source of fresh food.

The barbecue has become a much-loved, much-used and often sophisticated piece of equipment displayed on a deck, courtyard or balcony, whereas, back in the fifties and sixties, a barbecue was often home-made and a fairly primitive thing that was hidden away in a corner of the backyard and kept only for family use. While this cookbook has a nostalgic feel and look about it, the recipes are very 'today', they're quick and easy to make, they have that healthy but not worthy feel about them, they use lots of our wonderful fresh produce and a great variety of easy-to-get ingredients. Our recipes are mostly influenced by Asian, Middle-Eastern and European flavours; we're happy to adopt and adapt recipes and food styles from all over the world to make them our own. We wonder if, in another 50 years or so, these recipes will be called retro, too?

Pamela Clark

1

RISE & SHINE

FIFTY YEARS AGO, DASHING OUT THE DOOR WITH A
COFFEE, OR EATING CEREAL AT WORK, WAS SIMPLY
NOT DONE; IT WAS UNHEARD OF TO LEAVE
FOR WORK OR SCHOOL WITHOUT BREAKFAST.
THE TABLE WAS LAID, EGGS WERE COOKED, TOAST
WAS BUTTERED AND THERE WAS HOMEMADE JAM.
SO LET'S CELEBRATE THE ERA WHEN BREAKFAST
TOOK PRECEDENCE OVER THE TRAFFIC.

COOKED ENGLISH BREAKFAST

PREP + COOK TIME 20 MINUTES   SERVES 4

50g (1½ ounces) butter
300g (9½ ounces) button
  mushrooms, halved
8 chipolata sausages (240g)
4 rindless bacon slices (260g)
2 medium tomatoes (300g), halved
1 tablespoon vegetable oil
8 eggs

1 Heat butter in medium saucepan; cook mushrooms, stirring, about 5 minutes or until tender. Season to taste; cover to keep warm.
2 Cook sausages and bacon in heated oiled large frying pan. Remove from pan; cover to keep warm. Drain fat from pan.
3 Preheat grill (broiler).
4 Place tomato, cut-side up, on oven tray; grill tomato until browned lightly.
5 Meanwhile, heat oil in same large frying pan; cook eggs until done to your liking.
6 Serve mushrooms, sausages, bacon, tomato and eggs with toast, if you like.
NUTRITIONAL COUNT PER SERVING 47.7g total fat (20.2g saturated fat); 2424kJ (580 cal); 3.5g carbohydrate; 34.6g protein; 2.4g fibre

CLASSIC RETRO RECIPE

CLASSIC RETRO RECIPE

KEDGEREE

1½ cups (300g) white long-grain rice
415g (13 ounces) canned red salmon
80g (2½ ounces) butter
⅓ cup coarsely chopped fresh
     flat-leaf parsley
2 teaspoons lemon juice
3 hard-boiled eggs, chopped coarsely

1 Cook rice in large saucepan of boiling water until tender; drain.
2 Drain salmon; discard skin and bones. Flake flesh.
3 Heat butter in large frying pan; add rice, parsley and juice. Cook, stirring, until heated through. Add salmon and eggs; cook, stirring gently, until heated through. Serve with lemon wedges, if you like.
NUTRITIONAL COUNT PER SERVING 20.5g total fat (9.9g saturated fat); 1760kJ (421 cal); 39.7g carbohydrate; 19.1g protein; 0.6g fibre
TIP You can use leftover cooked rice, if you have some; you'll need about 5 cups.

SPINACH SCRAMBLED EGGS

PREP + COOK TIME 20 MINUTES   SERVES 4

20g (¾ ounce) butter
75g (2½ ounces) baby
 spinach leaves
8 slices pancetta (120g)
8 eggs
½ cup (125ml) light
 pouring cream
4 slices crusty bread (140g)

1 Heat half the butter in large frying pan; cook spinach, stirring, until just wilted. Drain on absorbent paper; cover to keep warm.
2 Preheat grill (broiler).
3 Place pancetta on oven tray; grill until crisp. Cover to keep warm.
4 Whisk eggs and cream in medium bowl until combined.
5 Heat remaining butter in same cleaned pan over medium heat. Add egg mixture; wait a few seconds, then using a wide spatula, gently scrape the set egg mixture along the base of the pan. Cook until creamy and just set.
6 Meanwhile, toast bread.
7 Top toast with pancetta, scrambled eggs and spinach.

NUTRITIONAL COUNT PER SERVING 25.7g total fat (11.7g saturated fat); 1559kJ (373 cal); 14.4g carbohydrate; 21.7g protein; 1.1g fibre

TODAY'S <u>BIGGEST</u> BREAKFAST BARGAIN!

Sweet LIVELY flavour! Deep-down goodness!

24 big breakfasts in every large packet!

No other corn flakes like them! No other *breakfast cereal* like them — because Kellogg's Corn Flakes are *alive* with the deep-down goodness of hand-picked, sun-ripened corn. Roasted, toasted and crisped, every golden flake rustles onto your plate. Such a sweet, lively flavour!

COMPLETE, SATISFYING BREAKFAST

Remember—Nutrition Experts say that one plate of Kellogg's Corn Flakes with milk and sugar plus bread and butter (or toast) gives you *one third* of your daily food needs!

SAVE MONEY — EVERY DAY!

Compare the cost of one serving of Kellogg's Corn Flakes with that of meat, eggs, fish and bacon these days! Only 30 seconds to serve Kellogg's Corn Flakes—no greasy grillers or pots to wash.

Something NEW and different!

"CORN FLAKE NUTTIES"

Your family will love these . . .

8 cups Kellogg's Corn Flakes; 4 ozs. peanut butter; 1 tin condensed milk; 1 teaspoon grated lemon rind; ½ teaspoon salt. Blend peanut butter with milk, salt and lemon rind.

Stir in Corn Flakes, mixing evenly. Place small portions on greased trays and bake in moderately hot oven for 15 to 20 minutes. Cool on trays. Store in airtight containers.

NEW PICTURE PACK

Kellogg's CORN FLAKES

CRISPER TASTIER

NET WEIGHT 16 OUNCES

ur family grocer recommends

Kellogg's **CORN FLAKES**

MILY'S DAILY NEEDS — ARE ON YOUR GROCER'S SHELF

November 4, 1953

BLT ON CROISSANT

PREP + COOK TIME 15 MINUTES SERVES 4

12 slices rindless shortcut bacon (420g)
4 large croissants (320g)
2 small tomatoes (180g), sliced thinly
8 large butter (boston) lettuce leaves
AIOLI
½ cup (150g) mayonnaise • 1 clove garlic, crushed
1 tablespoon finely chopped fresh flat-leaf parsley

1 Preheat grill (broiler).
2 Cook bacon in large frying pan until crisp. Drain on absorbent paper.
3 Meanwhile, make aïoli.
4 Toast croissants under grill about 30 seconds. Split croissants in half; spread aïoli over one half of each croissant then top with bacon, tomato, lettuce and remaining croissant half.
AIOLI Combine ingredients in small bowl; season to taste.
NUTRITIONAL COUNT PER SERVING 36.8g total fat (13.9g saturated fat); 2592kJ (620 cal); 39.5g carbohydrate; 31.4g protein; 3.8g fibre
TIP We used rindless shortcut bacon here, but you can use trimmed bacon rashers if you prefer.

BIRCHER MUESLI

PREP TIME 20 MINUTES (+ REFRIGERATION) SERVES 6

2 cups (180g) rolled oats • 1¼ cups (310ml) apple juice
1 cup (280g) yogurt • 2 medium apples (300g)
¼ cup (35g) slivered almonds, roasted • ¼ cup (40g) currants
¼ cup (20g) shredded coconut, toasted
1 teaspoon ground cinnamon • ½ cup (140g) yogurt, extra

1 Combine oats, juice and yogurt in medium bowl. Cover; refrigerate overnight.
2 Peel, core and coarsely grate one apple; stir into oat mixture with nuts, currants, coconut and cinnamon.
3 Core and thinly slice remaining apple. Serve muesli topped with extra yogurt and apple slices.
NUTRITIONAL COUNT PER SERVING 10.4g total fat (4.1g saturated fat); 1187kJ (284 cal); 37g carbohydrate; 8.2g protein; 4.3g fibre

POACHED EGGS AND SMOKED SALMON ON BLINI

PREP + COOK TIME 30 MINUTES   SERVES 4

8 eggs
200g (6½ ounces) sliced
   smoked salmon
2 tablespoons sour cream
1 tablespoon coarsely
   chopped fresh chives
BLINI
⅓ cup (50g) buckwheat flour
2 tablespoons plain
   (all-purpose) flour
1 teaspoon baking powder
1 egg
½ cup (125ml) buttermilk
30g (1 ounce) butter, melted

1 Make blini.

2 To poach eggs, half-fill a large shallow frying pan with water; bring to the boil. Break 1 egg into a small bowl or cup then slide into pan. Working quickly, repeat process with three more eggs. When all 4 eggs are in pan, return water to the boil. Cover pan, turn off heat; stand about 4 minutes or until a light film of white sets over each yolk. Remove each egg with a slotted spoon and drain on absorbent paper; cover to keep warm. Repeat with remaining eggs.

3 Serve blini topped with eggs, salmon, sour cream and chives.

BLINI Sift flours and baking powder into medium bowl; gradually whisk in combined egg and buttermilk until mixture is smooth. Stir in butter. Cook blini, in batches, by dropping 1 tablespoon of the batter into heated oiled large frying pan. Cook blini until browned both sides; you will have 12 blini. Cover to keep warm.

NUTRITIONAL COUNT PER SERVING 25.9g total fat (11.3g saturated fat); 1731kJ (414 cal); 14.1g carbohydrate; 31.5g protein; 1.6g fibre

breakfast makes a good start to the day. The modern trend
eakfasts, but it is wise to have some kind of well balanced meal
ng.

course fruit juice or grapefruit is a good choice, or perhaps one
-cooked cereals with milk, or try the Swiss dish Muesli, shown
site page.

weather porridge cannot be bettered for creating a feeling of
nd well-being.

MUESLI

1 tablespoon rolled oats
1 tablespoon sweetened
    condensed milk
juice ¼ lemon (optional)
3 tablespoons water
2 small or 1 large apple

Soak oats in 3 tablespoons of water overnight. Wash
apples and grate into bowl. Add condensed milk and
lemon juice. Muesli should not be left to stand — serve
at once or cover with a plate. Serve with fruit if wished.
For 1 person.

PORRIDGE

847

2 cups quick cooking
    rolled oats
5 cups milk or water
salt to taste

Add rolled oats (and salt to taste) to boiling milk or water.
Boil for 50 to 60 seconds, stirring continuously if using
milk. When water is used stir occasionally. Turn off
heat, cover and allow to stand for 5 minutes. Stir and
serve. For thicker porridge use more oats, for thinner
porridge use less oats. For creamier, smoother porridge,
boil for 2 or more minutes, stirring as necessary.

COOKING BACON

848

Bacon can be grilled or fried — be careful not to overcook
it for it is ready very quickly. Cut the rind off rashers and,
if frying, arrange in pan so that fat and lean overlap
— in this way you keep the lean part of the bacon moist.

SAUSAGE AND BACON

849

Cook sausages first — either grilling or frying these before
cooking bacon.

BACON AND TOMATOES

850

Cook tomatoes after bacon and eggs, since they tend to
make the pan sticky. When grilling, the tomatoes can
be put in pan under the bacon. Canned peeled tomatoes
are excellent with bacon.

BACON AND EGGS

851

Cook the bacon first and lift on to a hot dish. If nec
add a little extra fat — melt this, but do not get it t
or there will be a hard skin on the egg. Break egg
a saucer and slide into pan. Tilt pan slightly as ea
goes in to keep the white a good shape.

BACON AND MUSHROOMS

852

Fry bacon first. Add a little extra fat if necessar
cooking mushrooms or grill them in a pan whi
is on the grid.

BACON AND WAFFLES

853

Make a pancake batter (Recipe No. 636) bu
¼ pint liquid. Heat waffle iron and pour in bat
while grill or fry bacon.

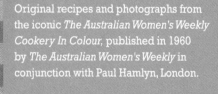

Original recipes and photographs from
the iconic *The Australian Women's Weekly
Cookery In Colour*, published in 1960
by *The Australian Women's Weekly* in
conjunction with Paul Hamlyn, London.

ZUCCHINI AND MUSHROOM OMELETTE

PREP + COOK TIME 20 MINUTES SERVES 1

10g (½ ounce) butter

1 clove garlic, crushed

25g (¾ ounce) button mushrooms, sliced thinly

¼ cup (50g) coarsely grated zucchini

1 green onion (scallion), chopped finely

2 eggs

1 tablespoon water

¼ cup (30g) coarsely grated cheddar cheese

1 Heat half the butter in small frying pan; cook garlic and mushrooms, stirring, about 2 minutes or until mushrooms are browned lightly. Add zucchini and onion; cook, stirring, about 1 minute or until zucchini begins to soften. Remove vegetable mixture from pan; cover to keep warm.

2 Whisk eggs and the water in small bowl. Add cheese; whisk until combined.

3 Heat remaining butter in same pan, add egg mixture; tilt pan to cover base with egg mixture. Cook over medium heat until omelette is almost set.

4 Place vegetable mixture over half the omelette; using spatula, lift and fold omelette in half over vegetable mixture. Carefully slide omelette onto serving plate.

NUTRITIONAL COUNT PER SERVING 11.7g total fat (6.1g saturated fat); 606kJ (145 cal); 0.8g carbohydrate; 8.9g protein; 0.9g fibre

EGGS BENEDICT

PREP + COOK TIME 40 MINUTES   SERVES 4

8 eggs
8 slices ciabatta (280g)
160g (5 ounces) shaved leg ham
2 tablespoons finely chopped
    fresh chives

MICROWAVE HOLLANDAISE

150g (4½ ounces) butter,
    chopped coarsely
2 egg yolks
1½ tablespoons water
1 tablespoon lemon juice

1 Make microwave hollandaise.
2 To poach eggs, half-fill a large shallow frying pan with water; bring to the boil. Break 1 egg into a small bowl or cup then slide into pan. Working quickly, repeat process with three more eggs. When all 4 eggs are in pan, return water to the boil. Cover pan, turn off heat; stand about 4 minutes or until a light film of white sets over each yolk. Remove each egg with a slotted spoon and drain on absorbent paper; cover to keep warm. Repeat with remaining eggs.
3 Meanwhile, toast bread. Top toast with ham, poached eggs, hollandaise and chives; season to taste.

MICROWAVE HOLLANDAISE Melt butter in microwave-safe jug on HIGH (100%) for 1 minute. Whisk egg yolks, water and juice in small microwave-safe bowl; cook, uncovered, on MEDIUM (50%), whisking every 15 seconds, for 1 minute or until thickened slightly. Don't allow the egg yolk mixture to boil. Add hot melted butter, a few drops at a time, to egg yolk mixture, whisking constantly, until mixture starts to thicken. Continue adding butter, in a thin steady stream, whisking constantly, until all butter is added and hollandaise is thick; season to taste. Cover surface of sauce with plastic wrap to keep warm.

NUTRITIONAL COUNT PER SERVING 47g total fat (25.2g saturated fat); 2817kJ (674 cal); 32.7g carbohydrate; 30.1g protein; 2g fibre

SERVING SUGGESTION Serve with rocket (arugula) leaves.

TIP If the hollandaise sauce splits or separates, place another egg yolk in a clean bowl and gradually whisk in the separated sauce, about a teaspoon at a time, until it's all incorporated.

RASPBERRY HOTCAKES WITH HONEYCOMB BUTTER

PREP + COOK TIME 40 MINUTES SERVES 4

2 cups (500ml) buttermilk

2 eggs

40g (1½ ounces) butter, melted

2 teaspoons vanilla extract

2 cups (300g) self-raising flour

¹/₃ cup (75g) caster (superfine) sugar

pinch salt

150g (4½ ounces) frozen
  raspberries, thawed

HONEYCOMB BUTTER

125g (4 ounces) unsalted butter,
  softened

¹/₃ cup (12g) finely chopped
  honeycomb

1 Make honeycomb butter.

2 Whisk buttermilk, eggs, butter and vanilla in medium jug until combined.
Sift flour, sugar and salt into medium bowl; gradually whisk in buttermilk mixture
until smooth.

3 Cook hotcakes, in batches, by dropping ¼ cup batter for each hotcake into
heated oiled large frying pan; sprinkle each hotcake with six raspberries. Cook
hotcakes until bubbles appear on the surface; turn, brown other side. Remove
from pan; cover to keep warm. Repeat with remaining batter to make 12 hotcakes.

4 Serve hotcakes with honeycomb butter.

HONEYCOMB BUTTER Beat butter in small bowl with electric mixer until light and
fluffy; stir in honeycomb. Set aside at room temperature.

NUTRITIONAL COUNT PER SERVING 40.1g total fat (24.9g saturated fat); 2922kJ (699 cal);
84g carbohydrate; 16.8g protein; 4.9g fibre

SERVING SUGGESTION Serve hotcakes with maple syrup and extra raspberries.

TIPS You can transfer the cooked hotcakes to an oven tray or heatproof plate,
cover with foil and place in oven preheated to 120°C/250°F to keep warm while
you cook remaining hotcakes.

Plain, uncoated honeycomb is available from speciality food stores, health food
stores, good delicatessens and confectionery shops.

BANANA RASPBERRY SMOOTHIE

PREP TIME 5 MINUTES   SERVES 1

½ small banana (65g), chopped coarsely
¼ cup (35g) raspberries
¾ cup (180ml) milk • 1 teaspoon honey

1 Blend or process ingredients until smooth.
NUTRITIONAL COUNT PER SERVING 2.7g total fat (1.7g saturated fat); 305kJ (73 cal); 9.4g carbohydrate; 2.7g protein; 1.1g fibre
TIPS You can use fresh or frozen berries for this smoothie. For an added energy boost, try adding half a coarsely crushed weet-bix to the smoothie; you may need to add a little extra milk if smoothie becomes too thick.

BERRY CROISSANT FRENCH TOAST

PREP + COOK TIME 30 MINUTES   SERVES 4

8 small croissants (400g) • 2 tablespoons strawberry jam
250g (8 ounces) strawberries, sliced thinly
1 tablespoon caster (superfine) sugar • 1 egg
¼ cup (60ml) milk • ½ teaspoon vanilla extract
40g (1½ ounces) butter

1 Using small sharp knife, carefully cut open the inside edge of croissants to make a pocket, leaving 1cm (½ inch) at each end. Spread jam in pockets; fill with sliced strawberries.
2 Whisk sugar, egg, milk and extract in shallow bowl until combined.
3 Heat half the butter in large frying pan. Dip four croissants, one at a time, in milk mixture; drain off excess. Place croissants in pan; cook until browned both sides. Remove from pan; cover to keep warm. Repeat with the remaining butter, croissants and milk mixture.
4 Serve croissants dusted with sifted icing (confectioners') sugar, and accompanied with extra strawberries.
NUTRITIONAL COUNT PER SERVING 33.8g total fat (19.2g saturated fat); 2416kJ (578 cal); 54.4g carbohydrate; 13.3g protein; 4.5g fibre

Yet another Australian Mother endorses MARMITE'S goodness

Marmite and peanut butter became popular sandwich spreads in the fifties and mothers' endorsements such as this were a favourite way of advertising them.
Advertisement featured in The Australian Women's Weekly magazine circa 1957

If you were to drop in on the Wiseman family, you'd meet three radiant young Australians — full of energy and bubbling over with good health. Mrs. Wiseman's secret? Every mother can share it — vitamin-rich Marmite every day!

Being a yeast AND vegetable extract, Marmite is a rich source of Vitamin B_1, the vital element needed for sturdy growth, sound nerves and abounding energy. Helps children get the full benefit of the other foods they eat too! A grand sandwich spread, Marmite will also add zest to your cooking. Just a little does a power of good as a drink and in soups, stews, gravies and broths.

"Preparing cut lunches is a daily job with me, and, nine times out of ten, the children specially ask for Marmite on their sandwiches," says Mrs. G. Wiseman of West Ryde. "I use it often in soups and gravies, too, for that tempting touch of flavour that my family love so much."

PROOF of Marmite's vitamin goodness is clearly printed on every label of this famous product. Essential to children, Marmite is equally valuable for elderly folk and convalescents. Sold by good grocers everywhere... Order it today!

MARMITE
Yeast and Vegetable Extract

CORN FRITTERS WITH SMOKED SALMON

PREP + COOK TIME 20 MINUTES   SERVES 4

¼ cup (35g) plain (all-purpose) flour
1 tablespoon rice flour
½ teaspoon baking powder
½ teaspoon mild or smoked paprika
¼ teaspoon salt
1 egg, beaten lightly
¼ cup (60ml) milk
1½ cups (240g) corn kernels
2 green onions (scallions), sliced finely
2 tablespoons finely chopped fresh
   coriander (cilantro)
cooking-oil spray
1 medium avocado (250g), sliced thinly
100g (3 ounces) thinly sliced smoked salmon

1 Sift flours, baking powder, paprika and salt into medium bowl; gradually whisk in combined egg and milk until mixture is smooth. Stir in corn, onion and coriander; season.
2 Spray heated large frying pan with cooking oil. In batches, drop 1 tablespoon of batter for each fritter into pan; cook until browned lightly both sides.
3 Serve fritters topped with avocado and smoked salmon.
NUTRITIONAL COUNT PER SERVING 15.3g total fat (3.6g saturated fat); 1154kJ (276 cal); 20.1g carbohydrate; 12.7g protein; 4.1g fibre
SERVING SUGGESTION Serve with lemon wedges.
TIP You will need to cut the kernels from two small cobs of corn for this recipe.

2

HORS D'OEUVRES

THE COCKTAIL HOUR WAS ALL ABOUT GLAMOUR. THE NEW MOOD FOR A GENERATION COMING OUT OF THE RESTRAINED POST-WAR ERA INTO THE FABULOUS FIFTIES WAS AS MUCH ABOUT RELAXING AS IT WAS ABOUT DRINKING. MARTINIS WERE THE COCKTAIL OF CHOICE AND THE FOOD — THE PRAWN COCKTAILS, THE DEVILLED EGGS — SERVED AT THESE GLAMOROUS OCCASIONS, REFLECTED THE FUN AND FLIRTATIOUS NATURE OF THE TIMES.

DEVILLED EGGS

12 eggs
2/3 cup (200g) mayonnaise
1 tablespoon dijon mustard
2 tablespoons each finely
  chopped fresh chives and
  flat-leaf parsley

1 Boil eggs in large saucepan of water about 6 minutes or until hard. Cool, then peel and halve each egg.
2 Carefully scoop egg yolks from whites into medium bowl. Place egg white halves on serving platter.
3 Mash egg yolks with mayonnaise and mustard until smooth; stir in herbs, season to taste.
4 Spoon egg yolk mixture into piping bag fitted with 1.5cm (¾-inch) fluted tube; pipe mixture into egg white halves. Serve devilled eggs sprinkled with extra parsley or chives.

NUTRITIONAL COUNT PER EGG 5.3g total fat (1.1g saturated fat); 284kJ (68 cal); 1.7g carbohydrate; 3.4g protein; 0.1g fibre
TIP Use a good quality whole-egg mayonnaise for this recipe.

CLASSIC RETRO RECIPE

PRAWN COCKTAIL

PREP TIME 30 MINUTES   SERVES 4

1kg (2 pounds) cooked
   medium king prawns
⅓ cup (100g) mayonnaise
2 tablespoons pouring cream
1 tablespoon tomato sauce
   (ketchup)
1 teaspoon worcestershire
   sauce
½ teaspoon Tabasco sauce
½ teaspoon dijon mustard
2 teaspoons lemon juice
8 baby cos (romaine)
   lettuce leaves

1 Shell and devein prawns.
2 Combine mayonnaise, cream, sauces, mustard and juice in small bowl; season to taste.
3 Divide lettuce between four glasses; top with prawns, drizzle with sauce.
NUTRITIONAL COUNT PER SERVING 13.2g total fat (3.9g saturated fat); 1070kJ (256 cal); 7.3g carbohydrate; 26.6g protein; 1g fibre
SERVING SUGGESTION Serve with lemon wedges.
TIP Use a good quality whole-egg mayonnaise for this recipe.

MARTINI

VODKA MARTINI

PREP TIME 5 MINUTES   SERVES 1

Place 1 small rinsed seeded green olive and a dash of dry vermouth into chilled 150ml (4½-fluid ounce) martini glass; swirl vermouth in glass to coat. Place 1 cup ice cubes and 45ml (1½ fluid ounces) gin in cocktail shaker; shake vigorously. Strain into glass.

PREP TIME 5 MINUTES   SERVES 1

Place 1 small rinsed seeded green olive and a dash of dry vermouth into chilled 150ml (4½-fluid ounce) martini glass; swirl vermouth in glass to coat. Place 1 cup ice cubes and 45ml (1½ fluid ounces) vodka in cocktail shaker; shake vigorously. Strain into glass.

ADAM'S APPLE

FRENCH KISS

PREP TIME 5 MINUTES   SERVES 1

Rub lime slice around rim of 150ml (4½-fluid ounce)
martini glass; turn glass upside-down and dip wet rim
into saucer of cinnamon sugar. Place 1 cup ice cubes,
30ml (1 fluid ounce) vanilla vodka, 30ml (1 fluid ounce)
green apple vodka, 120ml (4 fluid ounces) apple juice,
20ml (¾ fluid ounce) sugar syrup and 20ml (¾ fluid ounce)
lime juice in cocktail shaker; shake vigorously.
Strain into glass. Garnish with fanned apple slices.
TIPS You can buy cinnamon sugar from most supermarkets.
You can buy sugar syrup from bottle shops or you can make
your own. Stir 1 cup caster (superfine) sugar and 1 cup
water in small saucepan until sugar dissolves; bring to the
boil. Reduce heat; simmer, uncovered, 5 minutes. Cool.
Refrigerate in an airtight container for up to one month.

PREP TIME 5 MINUTES   SERVES 1

Place 30ml (1 fluid ounce) chambord (black raspberry
liqueur) and 30ml (1 fluid ounce) berry iced tea in a
chilled 1 cup (250ml) champagne saucer; stir gently.
Top with 120ml (4 fluid ounces) chilled lemonade.
Garnish with fresh raspberries.
TIP We used 'forest berry' tea bags to make the iced tea.

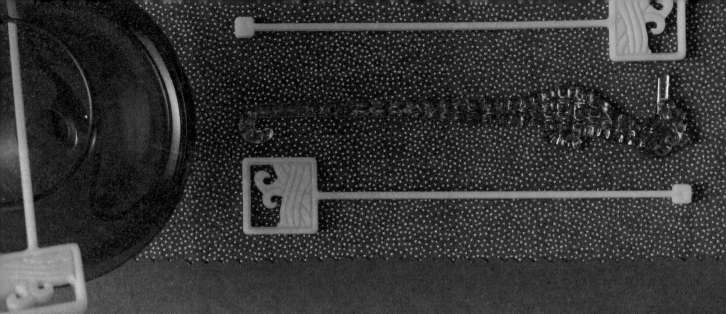

OOZY CHEESE FRITTERS

PREP + COOK TIME 45 MINUTES (+ REFRIGERATION) MAKES 72

60g (2 ounces) butter

1 teaspoon mustard powder

½ teaspoon sweet paprika

½ teaspoon chilli powder

⅓ cup (50g) plain (all-purpose) flour

1½ cups (375ml) milk

¾ cup (90g) coarsely grated gouda cheese

1 cup (100g) coarsely grated mozzarella
  cheese

4 green onions (scallions), chopped finely

¼ cup (35g) plain (all-purpose) flour, extra

¾ cup (75g) packaged breadcrumbs

2 eggs

vegetable oil, for deep-frying

MINT SALSA

1 cup loosely packed fresh flat-leaf
  parsley leaves

½ cup loosely packed fresh mint leaves

3 teaspoons red wine vinegar

½ teaspoon white (granulated) sugar

2 teaspoons rinsed drained baby capers

2 tablespoons olive oil

1 Melt butter in medium saucepan, stir in spices and flour; cook, stirring, over medium heat until mixture bubbles. Remove from heat, gradually stir in milk; stir over heat until mixture boils and thickens. Remove from heat, stir in cheeses until smooth; stir in onion, season to taste. Cover sauce, refrigerate about 3 hours or until firm.

2 Make mint salsa.

3 Place extra flour and breadcrumbs in separate medium shallow bowls. Beat eggs lightly in another medium shallow bowl. Drop rounded teaspoonfuls of cheese sauce into flour, coat lightly; shake off excess. Dip in egg, then in breadcrumbs; place on tray. Cover; refrigerate 30 minutes.

4 Heat oil in wok or deep, wide saucepan to 180°C/350°F. Deep-fry fritters, in batches, until golden brown; drain on absorbent paper. Serve fritters with salsa.

MINT SALSA Blend or process ingredients until smooth.

NUTRITIONAL COUNT PER FRITTER 2.9g total fat (1.2g saturated fat); 159kJ (38 cal); 1.9g carbohydrate; 1.3g protein; 0.2g fibre

TIP Make sure the oil for deep frying is very hot, only deep-fry the fritters for a few seconds, or they will break open.

Sizzling with tasty goodness!

From the Kraft Kitchen
"FRANKFURT-CHEESE SPECIAL"
— *a big, economical family meal*

"Every time you cook a main course dish with Kraft Cheddar, you save money," says Elizabeth Cooke. "For example, look at my 'Frankfurt-Cheese Special'. Here's a hearty, family dish — packed with nourishment. Kraft Cheddar is actually richer than sirloin beef in nourishing protein — and gives you additional food values you won't find in meat ... the essential vitamins A, B_2 and D, plus calories and those valuable milk minerals, calcium and phosphates. What a *bargain* in nutrition. So give your family this big, nourishing meal tonight."

"FRANKFURT-CHEESE SPECIAL"

4 medium potatoes;   1 medium onion;
3 tomatoes (tinned or fresh);   1 egg;
8 ozs. Kraft Cheddar;   3 frankfurts;
¾ cup milk;   Small rasher of bacon.

Chop bacon and onion and grate cheese. Peel and slice potatoes and tomatoes. Parboil the potatoes and the frankfurts for 5 minutes in salted water. Skin and slice frankfurts. Beat egg and add to milk. Grease a casserole and cover the bottom and sides with the well-drained potato slices. Sprinkle with the chopped onion, bacon, grated cheese, and season well. Add a layer of frankfurts and tomatoes. Repeat layers, saving enough cheese to sprinkle on top, and arranging extra potato slices around the edge. Pour beaten egg and milk into the dish and sprinkle with cheese. Bake in a moderate oven, 350°F. for 40 minutes or until it is set and the cheese brown on top. Serve with green peas and garnish with extra slices of tomato and frankfurt. Four generous serves.

KRAFT CHEDDAR

SOLD EVERYWHERE IN THE BLUE 8 OZ. PACKET OR FROM THE ECONOMICAL 5 LB. LOAF.

5
good reasons why Kraft Cheddar is best cheese value!

1   NO RIND—NO WASTE
2   FLAVOUR NEVER VARIES
3   SLICES EASILY — NEVER CRUMBLES
4   STAYS FRESH
5   PASTEURISED FOR PURITY

KFC-42

ALL YOUR FAMILY'S DAILY NEEDS — ARE ON YOUR GROCER'S SHELF

STICKY CHICKEN WITH PICKLED CUCUMBER

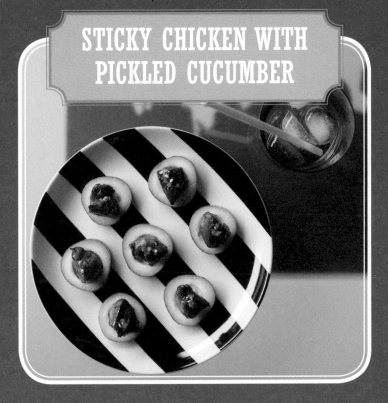

ASPARAGUS, TOMATO AND GOAT'S CHEESE TARTS

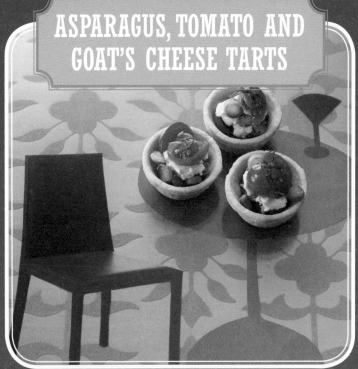

PREP + COOK TIME 40 MINUTES (+ REFRIGERATION) MAKES 30

300g (9½ ounces) chicken thigh fillets, chopped coarsely
1 tablespoon kecap manis • 2½ teaspoons white (granulated) sugar
1cm (½-inch) piece fresh ginger (5g), grated
¼ cup (60ml) rice vinegar • ½ teaspoon salt
4 lebanese cucumbers (520g)
1 fresh long red chilli, chopped finely

1 Combine chicken, kecap manis, ½ teaspoon of the sugar and the ginger in large bowl. Cover; refrigerate 30 minutes.
2 Stir vinegar, salt and remaining sugar in medium bowl until sugar dissolves. Cut cucumbers into 1cm (½-inch) slices; using teaspoon or melon-baller, remove and discard about half the seeds from each slice. Add cucumber to vinegar mixture, stand 10 minutes; drain on absorbent paper.
3 Cook chicken in heated oiled large frying pan until cooked through.
4 Top each cucumber slice with a piece of chicken; sprinkle with chilli.
NUTRITIONAL COUNT PER PIECE 0.7g total fat (0.2g saturated fat); 75kJ (18 cal); 0.8g carbohydrate; 2g protein; 0.2g fibre

PREP + COOK TIME 25 MINUTES MAKES 20

170g (5½ ounces) asparagus • 125g (4 ounces) cherry tomatoes
1 teaspoon finely grated lemon rind • 1 tablespoon olive oil
¼ cup loosely packed fresh basil leaves, shredded finely
20 shortcrust pastry cases
70g (2½ ounces) marinated goat's cheese, drained

1 Trim asparagus; slice thinly. Boil, steam or microwave asparagus until tender; drain. Rinse under cold water; drain.
2 Halve tomatoes; cut into thin wedges.
3 Combine asparagus and tomatoes in medium bowl with rind, oil and half the basil; season to taste.
4 Divide half the asparagus mixture into pastry cases; top with cheese, then remaining asparagus mixture. Sprinkle with remaining basil.
NUTRITIONAL COUNT PER TART 7.5g total fat (3.8g saturated fat); 485kJ (116 cal); 9.9g carbohydrate; 2.2g protein; 0.6g fibre
TIP You can use fetta cheese in place of goat's cheese.

SWEET CORN FRITTERS WITH ROCKET PUREE

PREP + COOK TIME 35 MINUTES   MAKES 48

1 egg
½ cup (125ml) milk
1 cup (160g) corn kernels
½ small red capsicum (bell pepper) (75g),
    roasted, chopped finely
½ small red onion (50g), chopped finely
1 tablespoon finely chopped fresh basil
½ cup (75g) self-raising flour
pinch bicarbonate of soda (baking soda)
½ cup (120g) sour cream
ROCKET PUREE
125g (4 ounces) rocket (arugula), trimmed
2 teaspoons olive oil

1 Make rocket puree.
2 Whisk egg and milk in large bowl; stir in vegetables and basil. Sift flour and soda over vegetable mixture, stir until combined; season.
3 Cook fritters, in batches, by dropping rounded teaspoonfuls of the vegetable batter into heated oiled large frying pan; cook fritters about 2 minutes each side or until browned.
4 Top each fritter with about ½ teaspoon each of sour cream and rocket puree. Serve fritters immediately.
ROCKET PUREE Bring a small saucepan of water to the boil. Add rocket, return to the boil; drain. Rinse rocket under cold water; drain. Blend rocket with oil until smooth; season to taste.
NUTRITIONAL COUNT PER FRITTER 1.5g total fat (0.8g saturated fat); 105kJ (25 cal); 2g carbohydrate; 0.7g protein; 0.3g fibre
TIPS We used corn kernels from 2 large fresh corn cobs in this recipe, but you can use frozen (then thawed) kernels or well-drained canned kernels.
Roast your own capsicum under the griller (broiler), or in the oven until the skin blisters and blackens; cover, cool, then remove skin before using. Or, buy roasted capsicum from a deli, or in jars.
A lightly oiled non-stick frying pan is ideal for cooking the fritters.

Make sure your bread is fresh, and the filling moist. Press top and bottom layer of bread firmly together so that the sandwich does not come apart.

By itself, a plate of sandwiches does not look very exciting. But garnishes can make all the difference. Instead of the conventional parsley try halved tomatoes, mandarins, oranges, watercress, prawns, cocktail onions, radish flowers — with suitable sandwiches all these garnishes look attractive and can be eaten too.

Serve a light white wine or fruit cup with a sandwich meal.

Original recipes and photographs from the iconic *The Australian Women's Weekly Cookery In Colour*, published in 1960 by *The Australian Women's Weekly* in conjunction with Paul Hamlyn, London.

HAT PINS

1055

8 oz. sausage meat

1½ tablespoons milk

3 teaspoons flour

½ teaspoon mustard
powder

3 cloves

rolled oats

For glazing:

2 tablespoons fruit juice

½ tablespoon vinegar

1½ tablespoons lemon or
orange juice

Mix sausage meat, rolled oats, egg and milk. Chill. Make approximately ... balls ... bake in ... ball ... dish for 30 minutes. **Drain** ... Cook for a few minutes or until slightly thickened. Dip the balls in the glazing. Fix on to cocktail sticks and allow to drain.

MINIATURE PANCAKES

1056

... hot until ready to ser...

SAUSAGE ROLLS

1057

6 oz. *flaky pastry*

8 oz. *sausage meat*
egg yolk or milk to glaze

Roll pastry into a ... Form the meat into a long roll and place down or ... and seal edges. Make slits across the top and cut into tiny rolls. Brush with milk or egg yolk and bake in a very hot oven for 15—20 minutes.

HOT BACON COCKTAIL SNACKS

Prepare these ... your guests arrive if you have no means of keeping them hot. Cook for 15 minutes in moderately hot oven, or 25 minutes if covered by foil. If you have a hotplate then just transfer them, when cooked, to a serving dish with absorbent kitchen paper underneath so you can prevent their being greasy, and keep on the hotplate so that guests can help themselves. Put firm cocktail sticks through centre of each roll. These snacks can be grilled or fried instead of being cooked in the oven.

Bacon Frankfurters

1059 Wrap small pieces of streaky bacon round cocktail Frankfurter sausages or portions of large sausages. For variety insert fingers of cheese or a small piece of crisp celery in the Frankfurter sausages. Grill.

Cheddar Fingers

1060 Wrap small pieces of bacon round fingers of Cheddar cheese, making certain the cheese is completely covered so that it is easy to eat. Grill.

DEVILS ON HORSEBACK

1061 Wrap small pieces of bacon round cooked prunes. If wished put a small piece of liver pâté in the centre of each prune. Grill.

ANGELS ON HORSEBACK

1062 Wrap small pieces bacon round seasoned oysters. Grill.

JAFFA ROLLS

1063 Wrap small pieces of bacon round segments of oranges. Brush with little butter before cooking. Grill.

ONION AND KUMARA PAKORAS WITH GREEN CHILLI YOGURT

PREP + COOK TIME 35 MINUTES   MAKES 80

2 cups (300g) chickpea (besan) flour

1 teaspoon ground turmeric

2 teaspoons ground cumin

½ teaspoon chilli powder

1 teaspoon baking powder

½ teaspoon salt

2 teaspoons kalonji seeds

2 medium brown onions (300g),
   quartered, sliced thinly

1 small kumara (orange sweet potato)
   (250g), grated coarsely

1 fresh long green chilli, chopped finely

½ cup (125ml) water, approximately

vegetable oil, for deep-frying

GREEN CHILLI YOGURT

1½ cups (420g) greek-style yogurt

2 fresh long green chillies, seeded,
   chopped finely

2 tablespoons finely chopped fresh
   coriander (cilantro)

½ teaspoon ground cumin

1 Sift flour, spices, baking powder and salt into large bowl; stir in seeds, onion, kumara and chilli. Gradually stir in enough water to make a thick batter; season.

2 Make green chilli yogurt.

3 Heat oil in wok or deep, wide saucepan; deep-fry rounded teaspoons of batter mixture, in batches, until browned. Drain on absorbent paper.

4 Serve pakoras hot, with yogurt.

GREEN CHILLI YOGURT Combine ingredients in medium bowl.

NUTRITIONAL COUNT PER PAKORA 0.7g total fat (0.4g saturated fat); 67kJ (16 cal); 2.3g carbohydrate; 1.1g protein; 0.6g fibre

TIP Batter will continue to thicken as it stands. If necessary, add a little water to thin it out.

LAMB ROGAN JOSH WITH ROSTI

PREP + COOK TIME 1 HOUR MAKES 48

2 teaspoons vegetable oil

1 medium brown onion (150g), chopped finely

1 clove garlic, crushed

1cm (½-inch) piece fresh ginger (5g), grated

600g (1¼ pounds) lamb backstrap, chopped finely

2 tablespoons rogan josh curry paste

2 medium tomatoes (300g), seeded, chopped finely

2 tablespoons lemon juice

2 tablespoons finely chopped fresh coriander (cilantro)

ROSTI

2 medium potatoes (400g)

40g (1½ ounces) butter, melted

1 Make rösti.

2 Meanwhile, heat half the oil in large frying pan; cook onion, garlic and ginger, stirring, until onion softens. Remove from pan.

3 Heat remaining oil in pan; cook lamb until browned. Return onion mixture to pan with paste; cook, stirring, until fragrant. Remove pan from heat. Stir in tomatoes, juice and coriander; season to taste.

4 Divide lamb mixture into rösti cases; serve immediately.

ROSTI Place unpeeled potatoes in medium saucepan, cover with cold water, cover pan; bring to the boil. Boil about 20 minutes or until potatoes are almost tender; drain, cool and peel. Coarsely grate potatoes into medium bowl; stir in butter. Preheat oven to 250°C/480°F. Press 1 teaspoon potato mixture over base and half-way up side of each hole in two 24-hole (1-tablespoon/20ml) mini muffin pans. Bake about 10 minutes or until browned around the edges. Remove rösti from oven, stand 30 seconds; then remove from pans, drain on absorbent paper.

NUTRITIONAL COUNT PER ROSTI 1.6g total fat (0.7g saturated fat); 134kJ (32 cal); 1.2g carbohydrate; 3g protein; 0.3g fibre

TIPS We used desiree potatoes, (a thin-skinned red potato) for the rösti. There is no need to oil muffin pans, unless they are scratched.

LAMB CUTLETS WITH DUKKAH

PREP + COOK TIME 35 MINUTES   MAKES 24

24 french-trimmed lamb cutlets (1.2kg)
1 tablespoon olive oil
DUKKAH
1 teaspoon cumin seeds • 2 teaspoons coriander seeds
2 tablespoons sesame seeds • ⅓ cup (45g) roasted hazelnuts
¼ cup (40g) whole blanched almonds • 1 teaspoon salt
½ teaspoon ground black pepper • ½ teaspoon sweet paprika

1 Make dukkah.
2 Brush cutlets with oil, cook on heated grill plate (or grill or barbecue) about 3 minutes each side. Transfer to a warm plate; cover, stand 5 minutes.
3 Spread dukkah onto large plate. Press one side of each hot cutlet onto dukkah just before serving.
DUKKAH Dry-fry seeds and nuts, separately, in small frying pan until fragrant and golden. Cool. Using mortar and pestle, grind seeds coarsely; add nuts, grind coarsely. Stir in salt, pepper and paprika.
NUTRITIONAL COUNT PER CUTLET 5.7g total fat (1.2g saturated fat); 314kJ (75 cal); 0.2g carbohydrate; 5.9g protein; 0.4g fibre

SCALLOPS WITH PEA PUREE

PREP + COOK TIME 30 MINUTES   MAKES 24

2 medium tomatoes (300g), peeled, seeded, chopped finely
1 tablespoon olive oil • 1 tablespoon verjuice
2 tablespoons fresh chervil leaves
2 teaspoons finely grated lemon rind • 24 scallops on the half shell
PEA PUREE
1½ cups (180g) frozen peas • ¼ cup (60ml) pouring cream
2 tablespoons hot water, approximately

1 Make pea puree.
2 Combine tomato, oil, verjuice, chervil and rind in medium bowl.
3 Remove scallops from shells; wash and dry shells. Spoon pea puree into shells.
4 Heat oiled large frying pan; cook scallops about 30 seconds each side or until browned lightly but still soft in the centre.
5 Place scallops on pea puree; top scallops with tomato mixture.
PEA PUREE Boil, steam or microwave peas until tender; drain. Blend peas with cream and enough of the water to give a thick pouring consistency; season to taste.
NUTRITIONAL COUNT PER SCALLOP 2.1g total fat (0.9g saturated fat); 167kJ (40 cal); 1.1g carbohydrate; 4g protein; 0.5g fibre

Munch them with *cheese*,
Crunch them with *ham*,
Spread them with *honey*,
Or serve them with *jam*.

...ten buttered
never bettered -

Only

Arnott's make
Sao Biscuits

There is no Substitute for Quality.

GREEN ONION BLINIS
WITH CHILLI CRAB SALAD

PREP + COOK TIME 40 MINUTES   MAKES 24

⅔ cup (100g) wholemeal plain
   (all-purpose) flour

¼ cup (35g) white self-raising flour

1 tablespoon plain (all-purpose) flour

½ teaspoon cayenne pepper

2 eggs

¾ cup (180ml) buttermilk

2 green onions (scallions), sliced finely

40g (1½ ounces) butter, melted

CHILLI CRAB SALAD

150g (4½ ounces) cooked crab meat

1 tablespoon each finely chopped fresh
   mint and vietnamese mint

1 teaspoon finely grated lime rind

2 tablespoons lime juice

2 teaspoons fish sauce

½ lebanese cucumber (65g), seeded,
   chopped finely

1 fresh small red thai (serrano) chilli,
   sliced thinly

1 Sift flours and pepper into medium bowl; whisk in eggs and buttermilk until smooth. Stir in onion and butter; season.
2 Cook blini, in batches, by dropping 1 tablespoon of the batter for each blini, into heated oiled large frying pan; cook blini until browned both sides. Cool on wire racks.
3 Meanwhile, make chilli crab salad.
4 Serve blinis topped with salad.
CHILLI CRAB SALAD Combine ingredients in medium bowl; season to taste.
NUTRITIONAL COUNT PER BLINI 2.1g total fat (1.2g saturated fat); 205kJ (49 cal); 4.6g carbohydrate; 2.5g protein; 0.6g fibre
TIPS You could serve the crab mixture on mini toasts, lavash or sliced french bread stick. You can buy cooked crab meat at the local fish markets or supermarket. Alternatively, buy fresh crabs and cook them (blue swimmer crabs are good). To tell if crabs are meaty, look at the claws; if they are pointy and sharp it means they have a new shell and don't have much meat. If the claws are rounded, they have an older shell and will have more meat.

Hors d'oeuvres

LOBSTER, HERB AND TOMATO ON WITLOF

PREP + COOK TIME 45 MINUTES   MAKES 48

2 uncooked lobster tails (500g)

1 tablespoon olive oil

40g (1½ ounces) butter

2 shallots (50g), chopped finely

1 clove garlic, crushed

½ teaspoon mustard powder

2 teaspoons finely grated lemon rind

1 tablespoon lemon juice

1 medium tomato (150g), seeded, chopped finely

2 tablespoons each finely chopped fresh flat-leaf parsley and chervil

48 red witlof (belgian endive) leaves

1 Turn tails upside down. Using scissors, cut down each side of the soft skin on the lobster tails. Peel away skin, remove meat from the shell. Cut into 5mm (¼-inch) cubes.

2 Heat 1 teaspoon of the oil and a quarter of the butter in medium frying pan; cook lobster, stirring, until changed in colour. Remove from pan.

3 Heat remaining oil and butter in same pan; cook shallot and garlic until soft. Remove pan from heat; stir in mustard, rind, juice, tomato, herbs and lobster. Season to taste.

4 Spoon lobster mixture into witlof leaves. Serve immediately.

NUTRITIONAL COUNT PER LEAF   1.2g total fat (0.5g saturated fat); 96kJ (23 cal); 0.2g carbohydrate; 2.4g protein; 0.9g fibre

TIPS   The same weight of prawns can be used instead of lobster. You will need about six witlof for this recipe.

3

The LUNCH ROOM

DURING THE FIFTIES AND SIXTIES, IT WAS COMMON FOR EMPLOYERS TO PROVIDE A LUNCH ROOM WHERE WORKERS GATHERED AT 12 O'CLOCK FOR THE LUNCH BREAK. LUNCH WAS USUALLY BROUGHT FROM HOME AND MOST OFTEN INCLUDED SANDWICHES MADE FROM LEFTOVER COLD MEAT AND SOMETHING FROM THE BISCUIT TIN. AT HOME, LUNCH WAS A POPULAR TIME FOR LADIES TO GET TOGETHER WHILE SCHOOL CHILDREN CAME HOME FOR A HOT LUNCH RATHER THAN STAYING IN THE PLAYGROUND TO EAT AS THEY DO NOW.

CURRIED EGG SANDWICHES

PREP TIME 30 **MINUTES** MAKES 16

6 eggs
⅓ cup (100g) mayonnaise
2 teaspoons curry powder
2 cups shredded iceberg
  lettuce
8 slices white bread (360g)

1 Boil eggs in large saucepan of water about 6 minutes or until hard. Cool, then peel and chop coarsely.
2 Use a fork to mash egg, mayonnaise and curry powder in medium bowl; season to taste.
3 Sandwich egg mixture and lettuce between bread slices. Cut crusts from bread; cut each sandwich into four triangles to serve.
NUTRITIONAL COUNT PER TRIANGLE
4.6g total fat (1g saturated fat); 448kJ (107 cal); 11.5g carbohydrate; 4.5g protein; 0.9g fibre

CLASSIC RETRO RECIPE

CLASSIC RETRO RECIPE

CORNED BEEF AND PICKLE SANDWICH

PREP TIME 5 MINUTES   MAKES 1

2 slices wholemeal bread (90g)

10g (½ ounce) butter, softened

2 tablespoons mustard pickles

2 slices corned beef (60g)

1 Spread both slices of bread with butter; spread pickles on one slice, top with corned beef, season to taste. Top with remaining bread slice. Cut in half diagonally to serve.

NUTRITIONAL COUNT PER SANDWICH
14.9g total fat (7.5g saturated fat); 1647kJ (394 cal); 41.9g carbohydrate; 19.7g protein; 6.3g fibre

TIPS You can use slices of leftover corned beef (page 164) or buy sliced corned beef from the deli. You can use your favourite pickle or other condiment.

PEPPERED RARE ROAST BEEF ROLLS

PREP + COOK TIME 35 MINUTES (+ COOLING) MAKES 8

1 tablespoon cracked
   black pepper
2 x 500g (1-pound) pieces
   trimmed beef eye fillet
1 tablespoon vegetable oil
½ cup coarsely chopped
   fresh flat-leaf parsley
¼ cup finely chopped fresh
   chives
2 tablespoons dijon mustard
8 long crusty bread rolls (600g)
40g (1½ ounces) butter,
   softened
2 tablespoons dijon mustard,
   extra
1 cup firmly packed trimmed
   watercress

1 Preheat oven to 200°C/400°F.
2 Sprinkle pepper over a sheet of baking paper;
roll beef in the pepper.
3 Heat oil in medium shallow flameproof baking
dish over high heat; add beef, turn until browned
all over. Transfer dish to oven; roast beef 20 minutes,
turning after 10 minutes for medium-rare, or until
cooked to your liking.
4 Remove beef from dish to plate; cover tightly
with foil. Cool.
5 Spread herbs over sheet of baking paper. Brush
beef with mustard; roll beef firmly in herb mixture.
Slice beef thinly.
6 Split rolls in half almost all the way through.
Spread butter, then extra mustard inside rolls;
fill rolls with beef and watercress.
NUTRITIONAL COUNT PER ROLL 16.4g total fat
(6.3g saturated fat); 1789kJ (428 cal);
34.1g carbohydrate; 34.4g protein; 2.8g fibre

TIP | BEEF CAN BE COOKED ONE DAY AHEAD. SLICE THE BEEF AS CLOSE TO ASSEMBLING ROLLS AS POSSIBLE.

CHICKEN, ALMOND AND TARRAGON MINI ROLLS

PREP TIME 20 **MINUTES** MAKES 6

Combine 1 cup finely shredded cooked chicken breast, 2 tablespoons finely chopped fresh tarragon, 2 tablespoons roasted slivered almonds, ½ finely chopped trimmed celery stalk, 2 finely chopped green onions (scallions) and 2 tablespoons mayonnaise in medium bowl; season to taste. Make a cut in tops of 6 mini bread rolls. Spoon chicken mixture into bread rolls.

NUTRITIONAL COUNT PER ROLL
6.4g total fat (0.7g saturated fat); 681kJ (163 cal);
17.6g carbohydrate; 7.7g protein; 1.9g fibre

PRAWN AND CAPER SANDWICHES

PREP TIME 30 **MINUTES** MAKES 16

Combine 150g (4½ ounces) cooked, shelled, finely chopped prawns (shrimp), 1 tablespoon rinsed drained, finely chopped capers, ½ cup mayonnaise, ½ teaspoon sweet paprika, 2 tablespoons finely chopped fresh flat-leaf parsley and 1 crushed garlic clove in medium bowl; season to taste. Divide prawn mixture between 4 slices of white bread; top with another 4 slices of bread. Trim crusts; cut each sandwich into four triangles.

NUTRITIONAL COUNT PER TRIANGLE
3.6g total fat (0.5g saturated fat); 393kJ (94 cal);
12g carbohydrate; 3g protein; 0.8g fibre

CHICKEN SALAD SANDWICHES

HAM, CHEESE AND TOMATO CHUTNEY WRAPS

PREP TIME 10 **MINUTES** MAKES 3

Combine 1½ cups finely chopped cooked chicken,
2 tablespoons finely chopped pecans, 4 thinly sliced
green onions (scallions), ¼ cup low-fat mayonnaise and
½ finely chopped trimmed celery stalk in medium bowl;
season to taste. Divide chicken mixture between 3 slices
of wholemeal bread; top with 60g (2 ounces) rocket
(arugula). Top with another 3 slices of wholemeal bread.

NUTRITIONAL COUNT PER SANDWICH

19.2g total fat (3.2g saturated fat); 1689kJ (409 cal);
30.9g carbohydrate; 25.4g protein; 2.9g fibre

PREP TIME 15 **MINUTES** MAKES 4

Place four mountain bread slices on board; top
each with a second slice of bread. Spread with
½ cup tomato chutney; top with 50g (1½ ounces)
baby spinach leaves, 2 cups coarsely grated cheddar
cheese and 300g (9½ ounces) shaved leg ham.
Season to taste; roll to enclose.

NUTRITIONAL COUNT PER WRAP

25g total fat (14.6g saturated fat); 2278kJ (545 cal);
43.7g carbohydrate; 35g protein; 2.7g fibre

TIPS Prepare the wraps the night before;
wrap each roll tightly in plastic wrap and refrigerate.
We cut our wraps in half to serve.

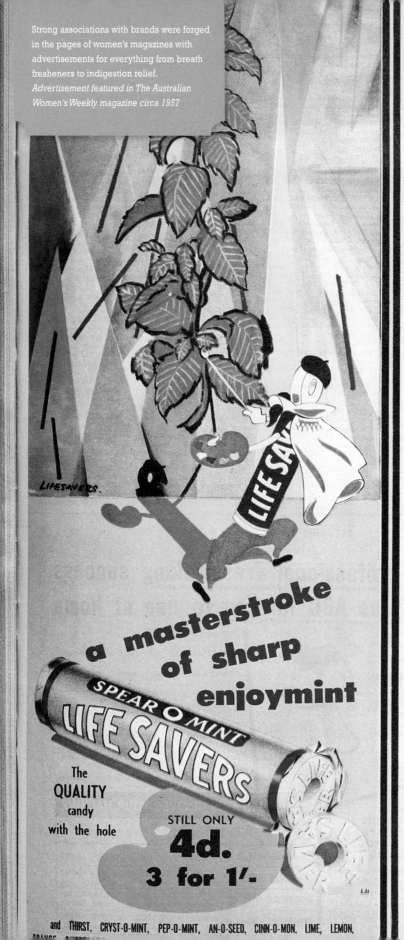

a masterstroke of sharp enjoymint

SPEAR O MINT LIFE SAVERS

The **QUALITY** candy with the hole

STILL ONLY **4d.** 3 for 1/-

and THIRST, CRYST-O-MINT, PEP-O-MINT, AN-O-SEED, CINN-O-MON, LIME, LEMON,

no fuss...
no mixing!
eat like sweets!

Wherever you are...

QUICK-EZE relieves **INDIGESTION** fast

PEPPERMINT FLAVOURED QUICK-EZE IN THE HANDY ROLL PACK

WALCO QUICK-EZE ANTACID TABLETS

FOR INDIGES
HEARTB
FLATULE
DYSPEP
ACID
NERVO
STOMA

7D EVERYWHERE

Famous formula gives 5-fold protection:
1. **Magnesium Trisilicate,** helps restore correct acid-alkaline balance.
2. **Calcium Carbonate,** gives rapid relief of pain and heartburn.
3. **Magnesium Carbonate,** relieves congestion in digestive tracts.
4. **Pure Oil of Peppermint,** has a sedative effect and relieves gastric and intestinal flatulence.
5. **Glucose** assists in the prevention of acidosis by raising the glycogen content of the liver.

LAMB WRAPS WITH BABA GANOUSH

PREP + COOK TIME 20 **MINUTES**   SERVES 4

500g (1 pound) lamb backstrap
1 teaspoon finely grated lemon rind • 1 tablespoon za'atar
1 tablespoon olive oil
4 pocket pitta breads (260g), halved
250g (8 ounces) baba ganoush
50g (1½ ounces) baby rocket (arugula) leaves

1 Combine lamb, rind, za'atar and oil in medium bowl; season.
2 Cook lamb in heated oiled large frying pan until cooked to your liking. Cover lamb; stand 10 minutes then slice thinly.
3 Spread inside of pittas with baba ganoush; fill with lamb and rocket.
NUTRITIONAL COUNT PER SERVING 33.2g total fat (18.4g saturated fat); 3352kJ (802 cal); 93g carbohydrate; 28.8g protein; 7.6g fibre
TIP Lamb can be prepared and refrigerated the night before; cook lamb and slice it in the morning, if you are taking the wraps for lunch.

SMOKED TROUT PASTA SALAD

PREP + COOK TIME 25 **MINUTES**   SERVES 8

340g (11 ounces) asparagus, trimmed
250g (8 ounces) penne pasta • ½ cup (150g) mayonnaise
¼ cup (60ml) lemon juice
½ cup coarsely chopped fresh flat-leaf parsley
1½ tablespoons rinsed, drained baby capers
2 green onions (scallions), sliced thinly
300g (9½ ounces) smoked trout, flaked

1 Cut asparagus into 5cm (2-inch) lengths. Boil, steam or microwave asparagus until tender; drain. Rinse under cold water; drain.
2 Cook pasta in large saucepan of boiling water until tender; drain. Rinse under cold water; drain.
3 Combine mayonnaise and juice in large bowl; stir in parsley, capers, onion, trout, asparagus and pasta. Season to taste.
NUTRITIONAL COUNT PER SERVING 8.3g total fat (1.2g saturated fat); 1003kJ (240 cal); 25.9g carbohydrate; 14g protein; 1.8g fibre
TIP The salad is best made and assembled the day you are going to eat it; it can be made in the morning if you are going to take it for lunch.

VEGETABLE SOUPS

CREAM OF MUSHROOM SOUP

8 oz. mushrooms*	2 oz. butter or substitute
1 pint water or stock	2 oz. flour
¾ pint fresh milk	seasoning

* The stems of mushrooms could be used if desired, and fried whole mushrooms added to the soup at the last moment as shown in the picture above

Chop mushrooms finely unless it is desired to strain the soup. Melt butter in saucepan, fry mushrooms for 5 minutes, stirring to prevent their discolouring. Stir in the flour and cook for 3 minutes. Remove the pan from the heat and gradually add water and milk. boil and cook until soup thickens. Season.

MIMOSA SOUP

49   *(See illustration below)*

Ingredients as Onion Soup Recipe No cookery section, but use twice as much liq

Simmer the soup for approximately ing, cover the top of the soup with by rubbing a soft cheese, such as E coarse sieve. Garnish with sprigs o

Original recipes and photographs from the iconic *The Australian Women's Weekly Cookery In Colour*, published in 1960 by *The Australian Women's Weekly* in conjunction with Paul Hamlyn, London.

LEEK AND POTATO SOUP

50

3 good-sized leeks
1¼ pints white stock or water
¼ gill cream or evaporated milk

1 lb. potatoes
1½ oz. butter or substitute
¼ gill milk
seasoning
parsley

To garnish: Duchesse potatoes piped into rings (Recipe No. 300)

Slice the leeks — using some of the green part to give a good colour — then heat the butter in the pan and cook the leeks for about 5 minutes, taking care they do not discolour. Add the sliced potatoes, stock and seasoning. Cook steadily for about 30 minutes. Sieve — return to the pan, adding the milk and cream, and re-heat without boiling. Pour into hot soup tureen and stir in a little extra butter, and chopped parsley. Garnish as illustrated.

CREAM OF TOMATO SOUP

51

1 lb. tomatoes
seasoning
cream (if wished)
2 oz. butter or substitute
2 oz. flour

1 gill water or white stock
1 onion
4 peppercorns
2 bay leaves
1 pint milk

Heat 1 oz. butter and sauté the sliced tomatoes and chopped onion together with bay leaves and peppercorns. Add water and simmer until quite soft. Rub through a fine sieve. Heat the other 1 oz. butter in a pan and stir in the flour. Cook for several minutes and gradually add the milk. Bring to the boil and cook until smooth and thickened — season well. Remember this is a thin white sauce. Reheat the tomato purée. Take both pans off the heat and make sure the contents are not boiling, then, using an egg whisk, whisk together. Add a little cream if wished. This method prevents the soup curdling.

CREAM OF TOMATO SOUP WITH CHEESE

52

Make the above tomato soup, but just before serving put a good layer of grated cheese on top.

Edam or Gouda cheese, with its mild flavour, is a very good accompaniment to this soup.

CHICKPEA, PRESERVED LEMON AND RISONI SALAD

PREP + COOK TIME 35 MINUTES   SERVES 4

250g (8 ounces) frozen peas
1¼ cups (275g) risoni pasta
1 tablespoon olive oil
2 cloves garlic, crushed
1 stalk celery (150g), trimmed, chopped finely
400g (12½ ounces) canned chickpeas (garbanzo beans), rinsed, drained
2 pieces preserved lemon (70g), trimmed, chopped finely
⅓ cup (55g) seeded black olives
115g (3½ ounces) goat's cheese, crumbled
YOGURT DRESSING
⅓ cup (95g) greek-style yogurt
1 tablespoon white wine vinegar

1 Boil, steam or microwave peas until tender; drain. Rinse under cold water; drain.
2 Meanwhile, make yogurt dressing.
3 Cook pasta in medium saucepan of boiling water until tender; drain. Rinse under cold water; drain.
4 Meanwhile, heat oil in large frying pan; cook garlic and celery, stirring, until celery softens slightly. Stir in chickpeas, preserved lemon, olives, pasta and peas. Sprinkle cheese over salad; drizzle with dressing.
YOGURT DRESSING Whisk ingredients in small bowl until combined; season to taste.
NUTRITIONAL COUNT PER SERVING 13.4g total fat (5.1g saturated fat); 2052kJ (491 cal); 66g carbohydrate; 21g protein; 10.4g fibre
TIPS Salad and dressing can be made a day ahead; store, separately, in refrigerator. It is best to store the dressing in a screw-top jar or small airtight container; drizzle dressing over salad just before serving.

POTATO AND GREEN BEAN SALAD

PREP + COOK TIME 1 HOUR 15 MINUTES   SERVES 8

6 medium potatoes (650g), unpeeled • 1 tablespoon olive oil
1 cup (180g) baby black olives, seeded
250g (8 ounces) green beans, trimmed, halved
THYME VINAIGRETTE
¼ cup (60ml) olive oil • 2 tablespoons white wine vinegar
1 clove garlic, crushed • 2 teaspoons fresh lemon thyme leaves

1 Preheat oven to 200°C/400°F.
2 Make thyme vinaigrette.
3 Quarter potatoes lengthways. Combine potatoes and oil in large baking dish; roast, uncovered, about 1 hour or until tender. Add hot potatoes and olives to thyme vinaigrette. Cool.
4 Meanwhile, boil, steam or microwave beans until tender; drain. Refresh under cold water; drain. Mix beans into potato mixture.
THYME VINAIGRETTE Whisk ingredients in large bowl; season to taste.
NUTRITIONAL COUNT PER SERVING 10g total fat (1.4g saturated fat); 711kJ (170 cal); 15.7g carbohydrate; 2.8g protein; 2.7g fibre

COS SALAD WITH BASIL DRESSING

PREP + COOK TIME 15 MINUTES   SERVES 8

4 rindless bacon slices (260g), sliced thinly
3 baby cos (romaine) lettuce, trimmed, leaves separated
BASIL DRESSING
⅓ cup each firmly packed fresh basil and flat-leaf parsley leaves
¼ cup (60ml) white wine vinegar • ¼ cup (60ml) olive oil
1 tablespoon wholegrain mustard • 3 ice cubes

1 Make basil dressing.
2 Cook bacon in heated oiled large frying pan until crisp; drain on absorbent paper.
3 Arrange lettuce leaves in large bowl, sprinkle with bacon, drizzle with dressing.
BASIL DRESSING Blend or process ingredients until smooth; season to taste.
NUTRITIONAL COUNT PER SERVING 9.9g total fat (2g saturated fat); 543kJ (130 cal); 1.5g carbohydrate; 7.7g protein; 1.6g fibre
TIPS Prepare bacon, lettuce and dressing in the morning; assemble salad just before serving. The ice cubes "hold" the colour in the dressing.

Munch them with *cheese*,
Crunch them with *ham*,
Spread them with *honey*,
Or serve them with *jam*.

Only **Arnott's** make **Sao Biscuits**

There is no Substitute for Quality

CHICKEN AND VEGETABLE SOUP

PREP + COOK TIME 2 HOURS 40 MINUTES (+ REFRIGERATION) SERVES 6

1.5kg (3-pound) whole chicken

1 small brown onion (80g), halved

2 litres (8 cups) water

5 black peppercorns

2 dried bay leaves

20g (¾ ounce) butter

2 stalks celery (300g), trimmed, sliced thinly

2 medium carrots (240g), cut into 1cm (½-inch) pieces

1 large potato (300g), cut into 1cm (½-inch) pieces

150g (4½ ounces) snow peas, trimmed, halved

3 green onions (scallions), sliced thinly

310g (10 ounces) canned corn kernels, rinsed, drained

1 Place chicken, brown onion, the water, peppercorns and bay leaves in large saucepan; bring to the boil. Reduce heat; simmer, covered, 2 hours.

2 Remove chicken from pan. Strain broth through colander into large bowl; discard solids. Allow broth to cool, cover; refrigerate overnight. When chicken is cool enough to handle, remove and discard skin and bones. Shred meat coarsely; cover, refrigerate overnight.

3 Heat butter in same cleaned pan; cook celery, carrot and potato, stirring, until onion softens. Skim and discard fat from surface of broth. Add broth to pan; bring to the boil. Reduce heat; simmer, covered, about 10 minutes or until vegetables are just tender.

4 Add snow peas, green onion, corn and reserved chicken to soup; cook, covered, 5 minutes or until hot. Season to taste.

NUTRITIONAL COUNT PER SERVING 9.2g total fat (2.8g saturated fat); 1183kJ (283 cal); 18.8g carbohydrate; 29.1g protein; 4.2g fibre

SERVING SUGGESTION Serve with crusty bread.

TIPS Soup can be made up to two days ahead; store, covered, in the refrigerator. If soup thickens a little on standing, add a little water or chicken stock. Reheat bowls of soup in the microwave or reheat soup in a saucepan on the stovetop.

CREAM OF KUMARA SOUP
WITH ROSEMARY SOURDOUGH

PREP + COOK TIME **40 MINUTES** (+ **COOLING**) SERVES 6

1 tablespoon olive oil

2 medium kumara (orange sweet
potatoes) (800g), chopped coarsely

1 medium brown onion (150g),
chopped coarsely

2 cloves garlic, quartered

2 teaspoons coarsely chopped
fresh rosemary

1 teaspoon finely grated lemon rind

2 cups (500ml) vegetable stock

2 cups (500ml) water

1 tablespoon lemon juice

½ cup (125ml) pouring cream

ROSEMARY SOURDOUGH

2 tablespoons olive oil

2 teaspoons finely chopped
fresh rosemary

1 loaf sourdough bread (675g),
cut into 3cm (1¼-inch) slices

1 Heat oil in large saucepan; cook kumara, onion and garlic, stirring, 10 minutes. Add rosemary, rind, stock and the water; bring to the boil. Reduce heat; simmer, covered, about 15 minutes or until kumara is soft. Cool 15 minutes.

2 Meanwhile, make rosemary sourdough.

3 Blend or process soup, in batches, until smooth. Return soup to same cleaned pan, add juice; stir over medium heat until hot. Season to taste.

4 Serve bowls of soup drizzled with cream, accompanied with sourdough.

ROSEMARY SOURDOUGH Preheat oven to 180°C/350°F. Combine oil and rosemary in large bowl; add bread, turn to coat in mixture. Place bread on oven tray; toast bread, both sides, about 15 minutes.

NUTRITIONAL COUNT PER SERVING 21g total fat (7.8g saturated fat); 2257kJ (540 cal); 69.1g carbohydrate; 15.7g protein; 5.6g fibre

TIPS Soup can be made up to two days ahead; store, covered, in the refrigerator. The soup is equally delicious simply served with thick slices of fresh sourdough to mop up the juices.

TIP WE SERVED THIS SOUP DRIZZLED WITH CREAM BUT IF YOU ARE TAKING THE SOUP TO WORK YOU CAN STIR THE CREAM IN, MAKING IT EASIER TO TRANSPORT.

4

The MILK BAR

ROCK AND ROLL, HAMBURGERS AND BANANA SPLITS — THESE ARE ALL SYNONYMOUS WITH ONE OF THE ICONS OF THE MID-20TH CENTURY, THE MILK BAR. WHAT BEGAN AS A CORNER STORE SELLING MILK AND GROCERIES, BY THE FIFTIES HAD BECOME THE PLACE FOR YOUNG PEOPLE TO GATHER AND ENJOY A RANGE OF DELIGHTS INCLUDING TAKEAWAY FOOD, NON-ALCOHOLIC DRINKS SUCH AS MILK SHAKES AND SPIDERS, AS WELL AS PIN BALL MACHINES AND, OF COURSE, THE JUKE BOX.

SPIDERS

PREP TIME 5 MINUTES   SERVES 4

8 scoops (480ml)
   vanilla ice-cream
1.25 litres (5 cups)
   creaming soda

1 Place two scoops of ice-cream in each of four 1½-cup (375ml) glasses; top with creaming soda.

NUTRITIONAL COUNT PER SERVING
6.4g total fat (4.2g saturated fat); 970kJ (232 cal); 43.8g carbohydrate; 2.1g protein; 0g fibre

TIP We used creaming soda but you can use any fizzy drink you like. Lemonade, cola, ginger beer, lime or orange would be nice.

CLASSIC
RETRO
RECIPE

BANANA SPLIT

1 cup (250ml) thickened (heavy) cream
4 medium bananas (800g),
   halved lengthways
4 scoops (240ml) chocolate ice-cream
4 scoops (240ml) vanilla ice-cream
4 scoops (240ml) strawberry ice-cream
4 maraschino cherries
1 tablespoon hundreds and thousands

1 Beat cream in small bowl with electric mixer until firm peaks form. Spoon mixture into piping bag fitted with large fluted nozzle.
2 Place two banana halves in each of four dishes; place a scoop of chocolate, vanilla and strawberry ice-cream between banana halves in each dish.
3 Pipe cream on top of each ice-cream scoop; top with cherries, sprinkle with hundreds and thousands.
NUTRITIONAL COUNT PER SERVING 33.3g total fat (21.8g saturated fat); 2236kJ (535 cal); 53.6g carbohydrate; 6.9g protein; 3g fibre

CORN AND GOAT'S CHEESE QUESADILLAS

PREP + COOK TIME 30 MINUTES SERVES 4

2 corn cobs (800g), trimmed
240g (7½ ounces) soft goat's cheese
8 large (20cm/8-inch) flour tortillas
½ cup (100g) char-grilled capsicum
(bell pepper), sliced thinly
40g (1½ ounces) jalapeño chilli slices,
drained
⅓ cup coarsely chopped fresh
coriander (cilantro)
20g (¾ ounce) butter
40g (1½ ounces) baby spinach leaves
1 lime, cut into wedges.

1 Cook corn on heated oiled grill plate (or grill or barbecue) until kernels are tender and browned lightly; when cool enough to handle, cut kernels from cobs.

2 Spread cheese over tortillas. Top four of the tortillas with corn, capsicum, chilli and coriander; season to taste. Top with remaining tortillas; press around edges firmly to seal quesadillas.

3 Heat butter in medium frying pan; cook quesadillas, one at a time, until browned both sides and heated through.

4 Serve quesadillas with spinach and lime wedges.

NUTRITIONAL COUNT PER SERVING 21.7g total fat (10g saturated fat); 2169kJ (519 cal); 57g carbohydrate; 19.8g protein; 8.6g fibre

TIP A quesadilla (from queso, the Spanish word for cheese) is a tortilla "sandwich" containing cheese and any of a wide number of spicy filling ingredients, which is grilled, fried or toasted and usually served with salsa.

BEER-BATTERED FISH AND CHIPS

PREP + COOK TIME **55 MINUTES**   SERVES 4

1 cup (150g) self-raising flour
1 cup (250ml) dry ale
1 tablespoon coarse cooking salt
(kosher salt)
1kg (2 pounds) potatoes
peanut oil, for deep-frying
4 x 150g (4½-ounce) blue-eye
fillets, halved lengthways
TARTARE SAUCE
⅔ cup (200g) whole-egg
mayonnaise
½ small brown onion (40g),
chopped finely
2 tablespoons finely chopped
cornichons
1 tablespoon rinsed, drained
capers, chopped finely
1 tablespoon finely chopped
fresh flat-leaf parsley
1 tablespoon lemon juice

1 Make tartare sauce.
2 Sift flour into medium bowl; whisk in ale and salt until smooth.
3 Cut potatoes lengthways into 1cm (½-inch) slices; cut each slice
lengthways into 1cm (½-inch) chips; pat dry with absorbent paper.
4 Heat oil in deep, wide saucepan; deep-fry chips, in three batches,
about 2 minutes or until tender but not brown. Drain on absorbent paper.
5 Dip fish in batter; drain away excess. Deep-fry fish, in batches, until
cooked. Drain on absorbent paper.
6 Deep-fry chips, in three batches, until crisp and golden brown; drain
on absorbent paper. Serve fish and chips with sauce.
TARTARE SAUCE Combine ingredients in medium bowl; season to taste.
NUTRITIONAL COUNT PER SERVING 38.3g total fat (6.2g saturated fat);
3340kJ (799 cal); 66.1g carbohydrate; 40.3g protein; 5.4g fibre
SERVING SUGGESTION Serve with lemon wedges.
TIP Reheat the oil between frying batches of chips and fish.

CAESAR SALAD

PREP + COOK TIME 45 MINUTES SERVES 4

½ loaf ciabatta bread (220g)
1 clove garlic, crushed
⅓ cup (80ml) olive oil
2 eggs
3 baby cos (romaine) lettuce,
    trimmed, leaves separated
1 cup (80g) flaked parmesan cheese
CAESAR DRESSING
1 clove garlic, crushed
1 tablespoon dijon mustard
2 tablespoons lemon juice
2 teaspoons worcestershire sauce
2 tablespoons olive oil

1 Preheat oven to 180°C/350°F.
2 Cut bread into 2cm (¾-inch) cubes; combine garlic and oil in large bowl with bread. Toast bread on oven tray until croûtons are browned.
3 Meanwhile, make caesar dressing.
4 Bring water to the boil in small saucepan, add eggs; cover pan tightly, remove from heat. Remove eggs from water after 2 minutes. When cool enough to handle, break eggs into large bowl; add lettuce, mixing gently so the egg coats the leaves.
5 Add cheese, croûtons and dressing to bowl; toss gently to combine.
CAESAR DRESSING Place ingredients in screw-top jar; shake well. Season to taste.
NUTRITIONAL COUNT PER SERVING 39.1g total fat (9.1g saturated fat); 2366kJ (566 cal); 33.1g carbohydrate; 18.4g protein; 5.6g fibre
TIP Named after Caesar Cardini, the Italian-American who tossed the first caesar salad in Mexico during the 1920s, this salad always contains fresh croûtons, crisp cos lettuce leaves, lightly boiled eggs, lemon juice, olive oil, worcestershire and parmesan, but no one ingredient should dominate.

237 CORNED BEEF CUTLETS

12 oz. can corned beef	dry breadcrumbs
1 cup breadcrumbs	fat for frying
seasoning	1 oz. butter or substitute
1 egg	1 oz. flour
	1/4 pint milk or stock

Make the sauce by heating the butter in the pan, stirring in the flour and cooking for 2 minutes, then adding the liquid. Bring to the boil and cook until thick. Add the breadcrumbs and the flaked corned beef. Season well. Form into cutlet shapes — coat with beaten egg and dry breadcrumbs and fry in hot fat until crisp and golden brown. Serve with fried tomatoes, peas and sauté potatoes. Garnish with cutlet frills.

Variation

Use 1/4 pint tomato soup or mushroom soup instead of milk. Add 1 — 2 chopped hard-boiled eggs or 1/2 cup diced cooked vegetables.

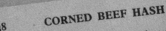

238 CORNED BEEF HASH

12 oz. can corned beef	1 oz. shortening for frying
approx. 8 oz. mashed	sliced beetroot
potatoes	parsley
1 egg	seasoning

Flake the corned beef and mix with the potatoes and beaten egg. Season well. Heat the shortening in a pan and put in the mixture. Spread this evenly and allow to cook slowly until the underside is golden-brown and the mixture really hot. Fold like an omelette and turn on to a hot dish. Serve garnished with beetroot and parsley.

Original recipes and photographs from the iconic *The Australian Women's Weekly Cookery In Colour*, published in 1960 by *The Australian Women's Weekly* in conjunction with Paul Hamlyn, London.

239 STUFFED BAKED MARROW

1 large can stewed steak
  and onions*
1 medium-size marrow
¾ cup breadcrumbs

good pinch sage
seasoning
2 oz. shortening

* or use 12 oz. cooked minced beef and 2 fried chopped onions

Tip the stewed steak and onions into a basin and cut the onions into smaller pieces. Add the breadcrumbs, sage and a little seasoning. Cut the end off the marrow and peel, unless it is very young when the peel can be left on. Fill the marrow with the mixture, replace the cut end in position, securing this with a skewer. Heat the shortening in a meat tin and turn marrow round in this. Then roast for 1 hour in a moderately hot oven. Cut into slices to serve and garnish with sliced tomatoes.

MOUSSAKA

240
1 large can stewed steak
little chopped parsley
¼ pint white sauce
  (Recipe No. 663)

approx. 12 oz. cooked
  sliced potatoes
2 skinned sliced tomatoes
3—4 oz. grated cheese

Arrange layers of potatoes in greased pie dish. Put the steak, sliced tomatoes and parsley on top of the potatoes. Cover with another layer of potatoes. Heat the butter, stir in the flour and cook for several minutes. Gradually add the milk and boil until thick and smooth. Stir in most of the cheese and seasoning and pour over potatoes, etc. Sprinkle with grated cheese. Cook for 40 minutes in moderately hot oven until golden brown on top. Garnish with parsley and sliced tomatoes.

241 CORNED BEEF LOAF

12 oz. can corned beef
2 hard-boiled eggs
2 cups breadcrumbs
1 onion

1 oz. shortening
1 egg
little milk
pinch sage
seasoning

Heat the shortening and fry chopped onion. Mix with flaked corned beef, breadcrumbs, seasonings, sage to a fairly dry consistency. Grease beaten egg and milk. Grease a loaf tin and coat with most of the breadcrumbs. Put in half the mixture, then arrange the 2 hard-boiled eggs and the rest of the corned beef mixture and greased paper. Bake for 45 minutes in a moderate oven. Turn out and serve hot with creamed peas and brown sauce (Recipe No. 6__) or cold with crisp salad.

CHEESEBURGERS WITH CARAMELISED ONION

PREP + COOK TIME 55 MINUTES   SERVES 4

500g (1 pound) minced (ground) beef

4 thin slices cheddar cheese (40g)

4 hamburger buns, split

8 large butter (boston) lettuce leaves

1 small tomato (90g), sliced thinly

4 large dill pickles (240g), sliced thinly

1 tablespoon american-style mustard

⅓ cup (95g) tomato sauce (ketchup)

CARAMELISED ONION

2 tablespoons olive oil

2 medium white onions (300g),
  sliced thinly

1 tablespoon light brown sugar

2 tablespoons balsamic vinegar

2 tablespoons water

1 Make caramelised onion.

2 Shape beef into four patties; cook on heated oiled grill plate (or grill or barbecue) until cooked through. Top each patty with cheese slices during last minute of cooking time.

3 Meanwhile, toast buns, cut-sides down, on grill plate.

4 Sandwich lettuce, tomato, cheeseburgers, pickle and onion between buns; serve with mustard and tomato sauce.

CARAMELISED ONION Heat oil in large frying pan; cook onion, stirring, until soft. Add sugar, vinegar and the water; cook, stirring, until onion is caramelised.

NUTRITIONAL COUNT PER SERVING 23.6g total fat (7.4g saturated fat); 2378kJ (569 cal); 51.6g carbohydrate; 34.9g protein; 5g fibre

TIP YOU CAN ALSO
USE CARAMELISED
ONION AS A PIZZA
TOPPING, OR AS
A FILLING FOR A
QUICHE OR OMELETTE.

CHICKEN BURGER WITH AVOCADO AND BACON

PREP + COOK TIME 40 MINUTES SERVES 4

¾ cup (50g) stale breadcrumbs

1 tablespoon milk

500g (1 pound) minced (ground) chicken

4 green onions (scallions), sliced thinly

2 tablespoons finely chopped fresh
 flat-leaf parsley

2 drained anchovy fillets, chopped finely

¼ cup (75g) whole-egg mayonnaise

1 clove garlic, crushed

1 teaspoon dijon mustard

1½ teaspoons lemon juice

4 rindless bacon slices (260g),
 cut into thirds

2 teaspoons olive oil

4 wholegrain rolls, split

4 baby cos (romaine) lettuce leaves

1 medium avocado (250g), sliced thickly

1 Place breadcrumbs in medium bowl; pour milk over breadcrumbs. Add chicken, onion, parsley and anchovies; season. Using hands, mix until well combined; shape mixture into four patties.

2 Combine mayonnaise, garlic, mustard and juice in small bowl; season to taste.

3 Cook bacon in heated oiled large frying pan until browned and crisp; drain on absorbent paper.

4 Heat oil in same cleaned pan; cook patties about 5 minutes each side or until cooked through.

5 Meanwhile, preheat grill (broiler).

6 Place bread rolls, cut-sides up, on oven tray; toast bread under grill until browned lightly. Sandwich half the mayonnaise mixture, lettuce, patties, avocado and bacon between toasted rolls; serve with remaining mayonnaise mixture.

NUTRITIONAL COUNT PER SERVING 37.3g total fat (9g saturated fat); 3076kJ (736 cal); 46.6g carbohydrate; 50.2g protein; 6.5g fibre

CHILLI AND MINT EGGPLANT BURGERS

PREP + COOK TIME 30 MINUTES   SERVES 4

¼ cup (35g) plain (all-purpose) flour
2 eggs
½ cup (85g) polenta
1 teaspoon hot paprika
1 medium eggplant (300g)
vegetable oil, for shallow-frying
1 loaf turkish bread (430g), quartered
8 large butter (boston) lettuce leaves
80g (2½ ounces) cheddar cheese,
   cut into 4 slices
½ cup loosely packed fresh mint leaves
⅓ cup (80ml) sweet chilli sauce

1 Place flour in small shallow bowl; beat eggs in second small shallow bowl; combine polenta and paprika in third small shallow bowl.
2 Discard top and bottom from eggplant; cut eggplant into eight slices crossways. Coat slices, one at a time, in flour, shake off excess; dip in egg then coat in polenta mixture.
3 Heat oil in large frying pan; shallow-fry eggplant, in batches, until browned lightly both sides. Drain on absorbent paper.
4 Meanwhile, preheat grill (broiler).
5 Halve each quarter of bread horizontally; place, cut-sides up, on oven tray. Toast under grill until browned lightly.
6 Sandwich lettuce, eggplant, cheese, mint and sauce between toasted bread quarters.
NUTRITIONAL COUNT PER SERVING 23g total fat
(6g saturated fat); 2684kJ (642 cal);
77.9g carbohydrate; 24.3g protein; 12.3g fibre

MUSHROOM RISOTTO

PREP + COOK TIME 1 HOUR 10 MINUTES   SERVES 6

3 cups (750ml) chicken stock
1 litre (4 cups) water
2 tablespoons olive oil
1 small brown onion (80g), chopped finely
10g (½ ounce) butter
2 cloves garlic, sliced thinly
100g (3 ounces) fresh shiitake mushrooms, sliced thinly
100g (3 ounces) button mushrooms, sliced thinly
100g (3 ounces) oyster mushrooms, sliced thinly
2 cups (400g) arborio rice
½ cup (125ml) dry white wine
75g (2½ ounces) baby spinach leaves
⅓ cup (25g) coarsely grated parmesan cheese
⅓ cup (50g) roasted pine nuts
¼ cup finely chopped fresh chives

1 Place stock and the water in large saucepan; bring to the boil.
Reduce heat; simmer, covered.
2 Heat oil in large saucepan; cook onion, stirring, until soft. Add
butter, garlic and mushrooms; cook, stirring, until mushrooms
soften. Add rice; stir to coat in mixture. Add wine; cook, stirring
until liquid is almost evaporated.
3 Stir 1 cup simmering stock mixture into rice mixture; cook,
stirring, over low heat until liquid is absorbed. Continue adding
stock mixture in 1-cup batches, stirring, until absorbed after each
addition. Total cooking time should be about 35 minutes or until
rice is tender.
4 Stir spinach and cheese into risotto. Remove from heat; stir in
nuts and half the chives, season to taste. Serve sprinkled with
remaining chives.
NUTRITIONAL COUNT PER SERVING 15.7g total fat (3.3g saturated fat);
1781kJ (426 cal); 55.2g carbohydrate; 16.8g protein; 3.3g fibre

The Milk Bar

Illustration featured in *The Australian Women's Weekly* magazine, circa 1957

COPPA AND RICOTTA PANINI

PREP + COOK TIME 30 MINUTES MAKES 4

⅓ cup (80g) black olive tapenade
¼ cup (60ml) balsamic vinegar
4 focaccia rolls (440g), halved • 1 cup (240g) ricotta cheese
½ teaspoon finely grated lemon rind • 1 teaspoon lemon juice
16 slices coppa (240g)
40g (1½ ounces) baby rocket (arugula) leaves

1 Combine tapenade with 2 tablespoons of the vinegar in small bowl;
spread over bottom half of each roll.
2 Combine cheese with rind and juice in small bowl, season to taste;
spread over tapenade.
3 Top cheese mixture with coppa and rocket; drizzle with remaining
vinegar then top with roll halves.
4 Cook panini in preheated sandwich press until browned lightly
and heated through.
NUTRITIONAL COUNT PER ROLL 18.2g total fat (6.7g saturated fat);
2036kJ (487 cal); 51.3g carbohydrate; 27.6g protein; 3g fibre

BANANA BREAD

PREP + COOK TIME 1 HOURS 30 MINUTES MAKES 12 SLICES

90g (3 ounces) unsalted butter, softened
1 teaspoon vanilla extract
1 cup (220g) firmly packed light brown sugar
2 eggs • 1 cup mashed banana
1 cup (150g) plain (all-purpose) flour
1 cup (150g) self-raising flour

1 Preheat oven to 180°C/350°F. Grease 14cm x 21cm (5½-inch x
8½-inch) loaf pan; line base and long sides with baking paper,
extending paper 5cm (2 inches) above long sides.
2 Beat butter, extract and sugar in small bowl with electric mixer
until light and fluffy. Beat in eggs, one at a time. Transfer mixture
to large bowl; stir in banana then sifted flours, in two batches.
Spread mixture into pan; cover with a strip of pleated foil.
3 Bake 40 minutes; uncover, bake about 30 minutes. Stand 5 minutes;
lift onto wire rack to cool.
NUTRITIONAL COUNT PER SLICE 9.5g total fat (5.6g saturated fat);
1296kJ (309 cal); 49.7g carbohydrate; 5.1g protein; 1.7g fibre
SERVING SUGGESTION Serve toasted or warm, with butter.
TIP You need two large overripe bananas (460g) for this recipe.

APPLE CRANBERRY PIE

PREP + COOK TIME 1 HOUR 45 MINUTES (+ REFRIGERATION)   SERVES 8

2 cups (300g) plain (all-purpose) flour

150g (4½ ounces) cold unsalted butter,
  chopped coarsely

½ cup (125ml) iced water

1 egg

1 tablespoon milk

1 tablespoon caster (superfine) sugar

CRANBERRY FILLING

½ cup (110g) caster (superfine) sugar

2 tablespoons water

300g (9½ ounces) frozen cranberries

APPLE FILLING

10 medium apples (1.5kg)

½ cup (125ml) water

⅓ cup (75g) caster (superfine) sugar

1 Process flour and butter until crumbly. With motor operating, add enough of the water to make ingredients come together. Turn dough onto floured surface, knead gently until smooth. Wrap pastry in plastic; refrigerate 1 hour.

2 Make cranberry filling. Make apple filling.

3 Preheat oven to 220°C/400°F.

4 Divide pastry in half. Roll half between sheets of baking paper until large enough to line deep 25cm (10-inch) pie dish; lift pastry into dish. Spoon cranberry filling into pastry case; top with apple filling. Brush pastry edge with combined egg and milk.

5 Roll remaining pastry until large enough to cover top of pie; press edges together with fork to seal. Brush with egg mixture; sprinkle with sugar.

6 Bake pie 15 minutes. Reduce oven to 180°C/350°F; bake about 30 minutes.

CRANBERRY FILLING Combine sugar, the water and cranberries in medium saucepan; simmer, stirring, about 10 minutes or until syrupy. Remove from heat; cool.

APPLE FILLING Peel, quarter, core and slice apples thinly; combine in large saucepan with the water. Simmer, stirring occasionally, about 10 minutes or until apple is tender. Drain apple; discard liquid. Stir sugar into apple; cool.

NUTRITIONAL COUNT PER SERVING 16.8g total fat (10.5g saturated fat); 1981kJ (474 cal); 72.2g carbohydrate; 5.7g protein; 4.9g fibre

TIP Both granny smith and golden delicious apples are suitable for this recipe.

SPICED ICED COFFEE MILKSHAKE

BANANA SMOOTHIE

PREP TIME **10 MINUTES**   SERVES 4

Place ¼ cup (20g) ground espresso coffee then ¾ cup boiling water in coffee plunger; stand 2 minutes before plunging. Pour coffee into small heatproof bowl with 2 bruised cardamom pods, ¼ teaspoon ground cinnamon and 1 tablespoon light brown sugar; stir to dissolve sugar then cool 10 minutes. Strain coffee mixture through fine sieve into blender or processor; process with 3 scoops low-fat vanilla ice-cream and 2½ cups no-fat milk until smooth.
NUTRITIONAL COUNT PER SERVING 1.6g total fat (1.1g saturated fat); 585kJ (140 cal); 21.2g carbohydrate; 9.7g protein; 0.8g fibre

PREP TIME **5 MINUTES**   SERVES 4

Blend or process 2 coarsely chopped large bananas, 2 cups milk, 1 tablespoon honey and 2 scoops vanilla ice-cream until smooth.
NUTRITIONAL COUNT PER SERVING 8.3g total fat (5.4g saturated fat); 911kJ (218 cal); 30.1g carbohydrate; 6.4g protein; 1.3g fibre
TIP Use overripe bananas for more sweetness; never use under ripe fruit because it doesn't puree.

HOT MOCHA

STRAWBERRY SMOOTHIE

PREP + COOK TIME 10 **MINUTES** SERVES 4

Heat 2 cups milk in medium saucepan, without boiling. Meanwhile, divide 100g (3½ ounces) dark eating (semi-sweet) chocolate among four 1¼-cup (310ml) glasses. Stir 2 cups hot black coffee into milk then pour mixture into glasses. Dust with 1 teaspoon sifted cocoa powder before serving.
NUTRITIONAL COUNT PER SERVING 12.1g total fat (7.5g saturated fat); 920kJ (220 cal); 21.9g carbohydrate; 5.7g protein; 0.4g fibre

PREP TIME 10 **MINUTES** SERVES 4

Soften 200g (6½ ounces) low-fat frozen strawberry yogurt slightly; cut into pieces. Hull 250g (8 ounces) strawberries; cut each in half. Blend or process yogurt, berries and 1 litre (4 cups) milk, in batches, until smooth.
NUTRITIONAL COUNT PER SERVING 10.7g total fat (7g saturated fat); 1012kJ (242 cal); 24.7g carbohydrate; 12.2g protein; 1.4g fibre

5

The
TEA ROOM

AFTERNOON TEA HAS NEVER REALLY GONE OUT OF FASHION, ALTHOUGH OLD-FASHIONED TEA ROOMS HAVE VANISHED, BEING REPLACED BY CAFES AND COFFEE SHOPS AS THE 20TH CENTURY MOVED ON. HOWEVER, THE DELICIOUS CAKES AND SANDWICHES SERVED IN THOSE TEA ROOMS ARE AS POPULAR TODAY AS THEY WERE A GENERATION AGO — INDEED, HIGH TEA TODAY IS A TRIBUTE TO THOSE GENTLE TIMES WHEN WE STOPPED FOR TEA AND CAKE IN THE AFTERNOON.

CUCUMBER SANDWICHES

1 telegraph (hothouse)
   cucumber (400g)
sea salt flakes
16 slices white bread (720g)
50g (1½ ounces) butter, softened

1 Peel and seed cucumber; slice as thinly as possible. Place cucumber in a strainer or colander, sprinkle with salt. Stand 20 minutes, then rinse cucumber with cold water; drain well. Pat dry with absorbent paper.

2 Spread bread with butter. Sandwich cucumber slices between bread slices.

3 Cut crusts from bread; cut each sandwich into three fingers.

NUTRITIONAL COUNT PER FINGER 2.4g total fat (1.2g saturated fat); 376kJ (90 cal); 13.7g carbohydrate; 3.7g protein; 1g fibre

TIP Use a mandoline or V-slicer to cut the cucumber into paper-thin slices.

NEENISH TARTS

PREP + COOK TIME 1 HOUR 45 MINUTES (+ REFRIGERATION & COOLING) MAKES 24

1¾ cups (260g) plain (all-purpose) flour
¼ cup (40g) icing (confectioners') sugar
185g (6 ounces) cold butter, chopped coarsely
1 egg yolk
2 teaspoons iced water, approximately
⅓ cup (110g) strawberry jam

MOCK CREAM
¾ cup (165g) caster (superfine) sugar
⅓ cup (80ml) water
1½ tablespoons milk
½ teaspoon gelatine
185g (6 ounces) unsalted butter, softened
1 teaspoon vanilla extract

GLACE ICING
1½ cups (240g) icing (confectioners') sugar
15g (½ ounce) unsalted butter, melted
2 tablespoons hot milk, approximately
pink food colouring
1 teaspoon cocoa powder

1 Process flour, sugar and butter until crumbly. With motor operating, add egg yolk and enough of the water to make ingredients come together. Turn dough onto floured surface, knead gently until smooth. Wrap pastry in plastic; refrigerate 30 minutes.

2 Grease two 12-hole (2-tablespoon/40ml) deep flat-based patty pans. Roll out half the pastry between sheets of baking paper until 3mm (⅛-inch) thick. Cut out 12 x 7.5cm (3-inch) rounds; press rounds into holes of one pan. Prick bases of cases well with a fork. Repeat with remaining pastry. Refrigerate 30 minutes.

3 Preheat oven to 220°C/425°F.

4 Bake cases about 12 minutes. Stand cases 5 minutes before transferring to wire rack to cool.

5 Meanwhile, make mock cream and glacé icing.

6 Divide jam between cases; fill cases with mock cream, level tops with spatula. Spread pink icing over half of each tart; cover remaining half with chocolate icing.

MOCK CREAM Stir sugar, ¼ cup of the water and milk in small saucepan over low heat, without boiling, until sugar dissolves. Sprinkle gelatine over remaining water in small jug; stir into milk mixture until gelatine dissolves. Cool to room temperature. Beat butter and extract in small bowl with electric mixer until as white as possible. With motor operating, gradually beat in cold milk mixture; beat until light and fluffy.

GLACE ICING Sift icing sugar into medium bowl; stir in butter and enough of the milk to make a thick paste. Divide icing between two small heatproof bowls; tint icing in one bowl with pink colouring and the other with sifted cocoa. Stir each bowl over small saucepan of simmering water until icing is spreadable.

NUTRITIONAL COUNT PER TART 13.6g total fat (8.8g saturated); 1016kJ (243 cal); 29.7g carbohydrate; 1.6g protein; 0.5g fibre

MINI CHICKEN AND LEEK PIES

PREP + COOK TIME 1 HOUR 20 MINUTES   MAKES 16

1 cup (250ml) chicken stock
170g (5½ ounces) chicken breast fillet
1 tablespoon olive oil
1 small leek (200g), sliced thinly
½ stalk celery (75g), chopped finely
2 teaspoons plain (all-purpose) flour
2 teaspoons fresh thyme leaves
¼ cup (60ml) pouring cream
1 teaspoon wholegrain mustard
2 sheets shortcrust pastry
1 sheet puff pastry
1 egg yolk
2 teaspoons sesame seeds

1 Bring stock to the boil in small saucepan. Add chicken; return to the boil. Reduce heat; simmer, covered, about 10 minutes or until chicken is cooked through. Remove from heat; stand chicken in poaching liquid 10 minutes. Remove chicken; chop finely. Reserve ¼ cup of the poaching liquid; discard remainder.

2 Heat oil in medium saucepan; cook leek and celery, stirring, until leek softens. Add flour and half the thyme; cook, stirring, 1 minute. Gradually stir in reserved liquid and cream; cook, stirring, until mixture boils and thickens. Stir in chicken and mustard; season to taste. Cool 10 minutes.

3 Preheat oven to 220°C/425°F. Oil eight holes in each of two 12-hole (2-tablespoon/40ml) deep flat-based patty pans.

4 Cut 16 x 7cm (2¾-inch) rounds from shortcrust pastry; press one round into each of the prepared holes. Spoon 1 tablespoon chicken mixture into each pastry case. Cut 16 x 6cm (2½-inch) rounds from puff pastry; top chicken pies with puff pastry lids. Brush lids with yolk; sprinkle with remaining thyme and sesame seeds. Using sharp knife, make two small slits in each lid. Bake, uncovered, about 20 minutes or until browned lightly.

NUTRITIONAL COUNT PER PIE 11.5g total fat (5.6g saturated fat); 740kJ (177 cal); 13.5g carbohydrate; 5.1g protein; 1g fibre

TIP Chicken mixture can be made the day before and kept, covered, in the refrigerator.

PRAWN WITH LIME AND PEPPER AIOLI SANDWICHES

PREP TIME 25 MINUTES MAKES 16

½ cup (150g) whole-egg mayonnaise
1 small clove garlic, crushed • ½ teaspoon finely grated lime rind
2 teaspoons lime juice • ¼ teaspoon cracked black pepper
16 medium cooked king prawns (shrimp) (720g)
30g (1 ounce) butter, softened • 8 slices white bread (360g)
1 cup (60g) shredded baby cos lettuce

1 Combine mayonnaise, garlic, rind, juice and pepper in medium bowl.
2 Shell and devein prawns; halve lengthways. Stir prawns into mayonnaise mixture; season to taste.
3 Spread butter over bread slices; top half the slices with prawn mixture and shredded lettuce then remaining bread. Discard crusts; cut each sandwich into four triangles.
NUTRITIONAL COUNT PER TRIANGLE 5.3g total fat (1.5g saturated fat); 518kJ (124 cal); 12g carbohydrate; 6.7g protein; 0.8g fibre

SALMON AND HERBED CREAM CHEESE SANDWICHES

PREP TIME 20 MINUTES MAKES 16

60g (2 ounces) cream cheese, softened
2 teaspoons each finely chopped fresh dill and chives
2 teaspoons lemon juice
1 teaspoon rinsed, drained baby capers, chopped finely
4 slices white bread (180g), crusts removed
125g (4 ounces) smoked salmon
4 large rocket (arugula) leaves, trimmed

1 Combine cream cheese, herbs, juice and capers in small bowl; season to taste.
2 Using rolling pin, roll over one slice of bread to flatten slightly. Spread with a quarter of the cream cheese mixture; top with a quarter of the smoked salmon and one rocket leaf, roll tightly to enclose filling. Repeat with remaining bread, cream cheese mixture, smoked salmon and rocket. Trim ends then cut each roll into four pieces.
NUTRITIONAL COUNT PER PIECE 1.9g total fat (0.9g saturated fat); 213kJ (51 cal); 5.2g carbohydrate; 3.1g protein; 0.3g fibre

Only **LAN-CHOO TEA** gives you this
DOUBLE ECONOMY

SAVE THIS LABEL

and share in the **LAN-CHOO BONUS PLAN**. There are over 400 useful presents to choose from.

U SAVE THAT EXTRA SPOONFUL

every time you make tea with LAN-CHOO. That's real economy!

LAN-CHOO
Ceylon's Choicest Tea

CHICKEN AND ALMOND SANDWICHES

PREP + COOK TIME 35 MINUTES (+ COOLING)   MAKES 24

1 cup (250ml) chicken stock

1 cup (250ml) water

6 black peppercorns

1 dried bay leaf

250g (8 ounces) chicken breast fillet

1 stalk celery (150g), trimmed,
   chopped finely

2 tablespoons flaked almonds,
   roasted

¼ cup (60g) crème fraîche

2 tablespoons whole-egg
   mayonnaise

1 teaspoon lemon juice

2 teaspoons finely chopped
   fresh tarragon

30g (1 ounce) butter, softened

8 slices light rye bread (360g)

1 Bring stock, the water, peppercorns, bay leaf and chicken to the boil in small saucepan. Reduce heat; simmer, uncovered, about 15 minutes or until chicken is cooked through, turning chicken halfway through cooking time. Remove chicken from poaching liquid. When cool enough to handle, chop chicken finely.

2 Combine chicken in medium bowl with celery, nuts, crème fraîche, mayonnaise, juice and tarragon. Season to taste.

3 Spread butter over bread slices; top half the slices with chicken mixture then remaining bread. Discard crusts; cut each sandwich into three finger sandwiches, then cut each in half crossways into squares.

NUTRITIONAL COUNT PER SQUARE 3.8g total fat (1.6g saturated fat); 343kJ (82 cal); 7.3g carbohydrate; 4.1g protein; 1.1g fibre

CREAMY EGG AND WATERCRESS SANDWICHES

PREP TIME **35 MINUTES** MAKES 16

3 eggs • ¼ cup (75g) whole-egg mayonnaise
1 teaspoon dijon mustard
1 tablespoon each finely chopped fresh chives and flat-leaf parsley
30g (1 ounce) butter, softened • 8 slices white bread (360g)
1 cup (20g) loosely packed watercress sprigs

1 Boil eggs in small saucepan of water about 6 minutes or until hard. Cool, then peel and mash.
2 Combine eggs, mayonnaise, mustard and herbs in medium bowl; season to taste.
3 Spread butter over bread slices; top half the slices with egg mixture and watercress then remaining bread. Discard crusts; cut each sandwich into four finger sandwiches.
NUTRITIONAL COUNT PER FINGER 4.9g total fat (1.7g saturated fat); 439kJ (105 cal); 11.1g carbohydrate; 3.7g protein; 0.8g fibre

RADISH WITH GREEN ONION BUTTER SANDWICHES

PREP TIME **30 MINUTES** MAKES 16

90g (3 ounces) butter, softened • 2 drained anchovy fillets, crushed
1 green onion (scallion), chopped finely
1 teaspoon dijon mustard • 12 slices white bread (540g)
10 trimmed radishes (150g), sliced thinly

1 Combine butter, anchovy, onion and mustard in small bowl. Season to taste.
2 Spread butter mixture over one side of eight slices of bread and over both sides of four slices of bread.
3 Top four slices of the bread buttered on one side with half the radish; top with the bread buttered on both sides. Top with remaining radish and bread. Discard crusts; cut each sandwich into four triangles.
NUTRITIONAL COUNT PER TRIANGLE 5.6g total fat (3.2g saturated fat); 527kJ (126 cal); 15.4g carbohydrate; 3.1g protein; 1.1g fibre

Illustration featured in *The Australian Women's Weekly* magazine, circa 1950

Original recipes and photographs from the iconic *The Australian Women's Weekly Cookery In Colour*, published in 1960 by *The Australian Women's Weekly* in conjunction with Paul Hamlyn, London.

SUBSTANTIAL SANDWICHES FOR HUNGRY FOLK

938 BACON BURGERS

hamburger (Recipe No. 1069)
8 rashers streaky bacon
French mustard

8 round soft ro...
tomato ketchup...
butter

Make the hamburgers as ingredients in Reci... but form into 8 thicker cakes. Wrap rash... round each, secure with cocktail stick. Fry... tender. Put between the buttered rolls, top... ketchup and serve with French mustard.

SANDWICH

...lespoon mayonnaise
...g to taste
...ndwich fillings**
... loaf

... slices,
... ress

... rd,
... a fish
... led

little
...d che...

chee...

tab...
...d c...

939 CRISP BEEF R...

1 large jar beef paste

ne...
b...

Cut thin slices of new bread. ... a generous layer of beef paste. R... Brush with melted butter or su... under a hot grill or in the oven. ... can be used instead.

940 DOUBLE DECKER SANDWICH

Spread slices of toast or bread with butter. Cover with crisp bacon and another slice of toast or bread. Butter this and top with fried egg and more bread or toast.

941 BACON WEDGES

Top thick slices of fresh bread with plenty
with crisp bacon rolls.

942 BANANA SURPRISES

thick fingers French banana butter (Recipe
 bread   No. 943)
bananas

Make a hole in the middle of each piece of French bread. Spread with banana butter, and put a portion of banana through. Children love these.

943 BANANA BUTTER

2 oz. butter   squeeze lemon juice
1 large banana

Cream the butter in a basin or on a saucer, and gradually mash the banana into this. Add a squeeze of lemon.

944 SARDINE FINGERS

French bread   sardines
savoury butter (Recipe lemon
 No. 945)   parsley

Make savoury butter and spread generously over thick fingers of French bread. Put the sardines on top and garnish with lemon and parsley.

945 SAVOURY BUTTER

2 oz. butter   good pinch celery salt
squeeze lemon juice good pinch cayenne pepper

Mix all the ingredients together.

LEMON CREME BRULEE TARTS

PREP + COOK TIME 1 HOUR 10 MINUTES (+ REFRIGERATION & COOLING) MAKES 24

1¼ cups (310ml) pouring cream
⅓ cup (80ml) milk
4 x 5cm (2-inch) strips lemon rind
4 egg yolks
¼ cup (55g) caster (superfine) sugar
PASTRY
1¾ cups (260g) plain (all-purpose) flour
¼ cup (40g) icing (confectioners') sugar
2 teaspoons finely grated lemon rind
185g (6 ounces) cold butter,
  chopped coarsely
1 egg yolk
2 teaspoons iced water, approximately
TOFFEE
1 cup (220g) caster (superfine) sugar
½ cup (125ml) water

1 Make pastry.
2 Grease two 12-hole (1½-tablespoons/30ml) shallow round-based patty pans. Roll half the pastry between sheets of baking paper to 3mm (⅛-inch) thickness. Cut 12 x 6cm (2¼-inch) fluted rounds from pastry; press rounds into holes in pans. Repeat with remaining pastry. Refrigerate 30 minutes.
3 Preheat oven to 160°C/325°F.
4 Bring cream, milk and rind to the boil in small saucepan. Beat egg yolks and sugar in small bowl with electric mixer until thick and creamy. Gradually beat hot cream mixture into egg mixture; allow bubbles to subside. Strain custard into medium jug, pour into cases.
5 Bake tarts about 25 minutes. Cool. Refrigerate 2 hours.
6 Make toffee.
7 Remove tarts from pan; place on oven tray. Sprinkle custard with toffee; using blowtorch, heat until toffee caramelises.
PASTRY Process flour, sugar, rind and butter until crumbly. With motor operating, add egg yolk and enough of the water to make ingredients come together. Turn dough onto floured surface, knead gently until smooth. Wrap pastry in plastic; refrigerate 30 minutes.
TOFFEE Stir sugar and the water in medium saucepan over heat, without boiling, until sugar dissolves. Bring to the boil. Boil, uncovered, without stirring, until golden brown. Pour toffee on greased oven tray to set. Break toffee into large pieces; process until chopped finely.
NUTRITIONAL COUNT PER TART 13.3g total fat (8.4g saturated fat); 702kJ (168 cal); 21.5g carbohydrate; 2.2g protein; 0.4g fibre
TIPS It is fine to use just one 300ml carton of cream for this recipe. Blowtorches are available from kitchenware and hardware stores.

CHERRY BAKEWELL TARTS

PREP + COOK TIME 1 HOUR (+ REFRIGERATION & COOLING)   MAKES 24

90g (3 ounces) unsalted butter, softened
2 tablespoons caster (superfine) sugar
1 egg yolk
1 cup (150g) plain (all-purpose) flour
½ cup (60g) ground almonds
2 tablespoons strawberry jam
12 red glacé cherries, halved

ALMOND FILLING

125g (4 ounces) unsalted butter, softened
½ teaspoon finely grated lemon rind
½ cup (110g) caster (superfine) sugar
2 eggs
¾ cup (90g) ground almonds
2 tablespoons plain (all-purpose) flour

LEMON GLAZE

1 cup (160g) icing (confectioners') sugar
2 tablespoons lemon juice, approximately

1 Beat butter, sugar and egg yolk in small bowl with electric mixer until combined. Stir in sifted flour and ground almonds, in two batches. Turn dough onto floured surface, knead gently until smooth. Wrap pastry in plastic; refrigerate 30 minutes.
2 Preheat oven to 220°C/425°F.
3 Make almond filling.
4 Grease two 12-hole (1½-tablespoon/30ml) shallow round-based patty pans. Roll pastry between sheets of baking paper until 3mm (⅛ inch) thick. Cut 24 x 6cm (2¼-inch) rounds from pastry; press rounds into holes in pans. Spoon jam then filling into cases.
5 Bake tarts about 20 minutes. Stand 10 minutes in pans; turn, top-side up, onto wire rack.
6 Meanwhile, make lemon glaze.
7 Spoon glaze over warm tarts; top with cherries, then cool.

ALMOND FILLING Beat butter, rind and sugar in small bowl with electric mixer until light and fluffy. Beat in eggs, one at a time. Stir in ground almonds and flour.

LEMON GLAZE Sift icing sugar into small bowl, stir in enough juice to make glaze pourable.

NUTRITIONAL COUNT PER TART 11.4g total fat (5.2g saturated fat); 748kJ (179 cal); 21.1g carbohydrate; 2.8g protein; 0.9g fibre

COCONUT FRENCH MACAROONS

PREP + COOK TIME 45 MINUTES (+ STANDING) **MAKES** 16

3 egg whites
¼ cup (55g) caster (superfine) sugar
½ teaspoon coconut essence
1¼ cups (200g) icing (confectioners') sugar
¾ cup (90g) ground almonds
¼ cup (20g) desiccated coconut
1 tablespoon icing (confectioners') sugar, extra
WHITE CHOCOLATE GANACHE
¼ cup (60ml) pouring cream
155g (5 ounces) white eating chocolate, chopped coarsely
2 teaspoons coconut-flavoured liqueur

1 Preheat oven to 150°C/300°F. Grease oven trays; line with baking paper.
2 Beat egg whites in small bowl with electric mixer until soft peaks form. Add caster sugar and essence, beat until sugar dissolves; transfer mixture to large bowl. Fold in sifted icing sugar, ground almonds and coconut, in two batches.
3 Spoon mixture into piping bag fitted with 1cm (½-inch) plain tube. Pipe 4cm (1½-inch) rounds about 2.5cm (1 inch) apart onto trays. Tap trays on bench so macaroons spread slightly. Stand 30 minutes.
4 Bake macaroons about 20 minutes. Cool on trays.
5 Meanwhile, make white chocolate ganache.
6 Sandwich macaroons with ganache. Serve dusted with extra sifted icing sugar.
WHITE CHOCOLATE GANACHE Bring cream to the boil in small saucepan. Remove from heat; pour over chocolate in small heatproof bowl, stir until smooth. Stir in liqueur. Stand at room temperature until spreadable.
NUTRITIONAL COUNT PER MACAROON 8.8g total fat (4g saturated fat); 686kJ (164 cal); 22.6g carbohydrate; 2.6g protein; 0.7g fibre

MASCARPONE AND PAPAYA TARTS

PREP + COOK TIME 55 MINUTES (+ REFRIGERATION & COOLING) MAKES 24

1¾ cups (260g) plain (all-purpose) flour
¼ cup (40g) icing (confectioners') sugar
185g (6 ounces) cold butter, chopped coarsely
2 tablespoons finely chopped glacé ginger
1 egg yolk
2 teaspoons iced water, approximately
½ small papaya (325g), seeded

MASCARPONE FILLING
250g (8 ounces) mascarpone cheese
⅓ cup (80ml) thickened (heavy) cream
2 tablespoons honey
¼ cup (70g) mashed papaya
1 tablespoon lime juice

1 Process flour, sugar, butter and ginger until crumbly. With motor operating, add egg yolk and enough of the water to make ingredients come together. Turn dough onto floured surface, knead gently until smooth. Wrap pastry in plastic; refrigerate 30 minutes.
2 Grease two 12-hole (2-tablespoon/40ml) deep flat-based patty pans. Roll out half the pastry between sheets of baking paper until 3mm (⅛-inch) thick. Cut 12 x 7.5cm (3-inch) rounds from pastry; press pastry rounds into holes of one pan. Prick base of cases well with a fork. Repeat with remaining pastry. Refrigerate 30 minutes.
3 Preheat oven to 220°C/425°F.
4 Bake cases about 12 minutes. Stand cases 5 minutes; transfer to wire rack to cool.
5 Meanwhile, make mascarpone filling.
6 Using vegetable peeler, slice papaya into small thin strips. Divide mascarpone filling into cases; top with papaya.
MASCARPONE FILLING Beat mascarpone, cream and honey in small bowl with electric mixer until smooth. Fold in papaya and juice.
NUTRITIONAL COUNT PER TART 13.9g total fat (9g saturated fat); 773kJ (185 cal); 13.5g carbohydrate; 1.6g protein; 0.8g fibre
TIP You will need 1 small papaya (650g) for this recipe.

SCONES WITH JAM AND CREAM

PREP + COOK TIME 35 MINUTES MAKES 25

2½ cups (375g) self-raising flour
1 tablespoon caster (superfine) sugar
30g (1 ounce) butter, chopped • 1¼ cups (310ml) buttermilk
¾ cup (240g) black cherry jam
1 cup (250ml) thick (double) cream

1 Preheat oven to 220°C/425°F. Grease 22cm (9-inch) square cake pan.
2 Sift flour and sugar into large bowl; rub in butter.
3 Add buttermilk. Use a knife to cut the buttermilk through the flour mixture to make a soft, sticky dough. Turn dough onto floured surface, knead gently until smooth.
4 Press dough out to 2cm (¾ inch) thickness, cut out 4cm (1½-inch) rounds. Place scones, just touching, in pan. Gently knead scraps of dough together; repeat process. Brush scones with a little extra buttermilk.
5 Bake scones about 15 minutes. Serve warm scones with jam and cream.
NUTRITIONAL COUNT PER SCONE 6.4g total fat (4g saturated fat); 589kJ (141 cal); 18.4g carbohydrate; 2.2g protein; 0.7g fibre
TIPS Scones are best made on the day of serving.
You can replace the thick (double) cream with clotted cream or whipped thickened (heavy) cream.

ROSEWATER MERINGUES

PREP + COOK TIME 1 HOUR 30 MINUTES (+ COOLING)
MAKES 50

3 egg whites • ¾ cup (165g) caster (superfine) sugar
2 teaspoons rosewater
1¼ cups (310ml) thickened (heavy) cream
50g (1½ ounces) rose persian fairy floss

1 Preheat oven to 120°C/250°F. Grease oven trays; line with baking paper.
2 Beat egg whites in small bowl with electric mixer until soft peaks form. Gradually add sugar, one tablespoon at a time, beating until sugar dissolves between additions. Fold in rosewater.
3 Drop heaped tablespoons of meringue mixture, about 5cm (2 inches) apart, onto trays; bake about 1 hour. Cool in oven with door ajar.
4 Meanwhile, beat cream in small bowl with electric mixer until soft peaks form.
5 Top meringues with cream and fairy floss. Sprinkle with pink rose petals, if you like.
NUTRITIONAL COUNT PER MERINGUE 9.3g total fat (6.1g saturated fat); 665kJ (159 cal); 18.6g carbohydrate; 1.4g protein; 0g fibre
TIP Persian fairy floss is available from gourmet food stores.
Use regular pink fairy floss if you can't find the persian variety.

Isn't it gorgeous?

The polka dot cake you make so easily with Puffin Cake Mix!

Puffin Cake Mix

JUST ADD EGGS AND MILK — YOU'LL MAKE A PERFECT CAKE

NOW Easier than ever to make!

"Everyone loves layer cake! Make it specially delicious and gay with colourful chocolate buttons!" says *Betty King*
Home Economist of World Brands

This is the kind of cake you'll be proud to bring in — a high-rising, light, rich-flavoured layer cake that stays deliciously fresh to the very last slice. You make it in minutes — without weighing, creaming or tiring beating. Only *one* bowl needed. With Puffin Cake Mix, all the *hard* work has been done for you before you open the pack!

From packet to oven in minutes with this recipe!
You just add eggs and milk to Puffin Cake Mix, and bake. Then sandwich those fine, moist-textured layers with your favourite icing and frost all over. (Four easy frostings to choose from, on the pack!) Now, press those little chocolate buttons all over (we've used Cadbury's Dairy Milk Rolls). Finished! Quickest cake you've ever made!

Special ingredients in Puffin guarantee success.
You see, Puffin contains special soft flour and enriched shortening you can't buy in any other way. These ingredients are blended accurately and smoothly with fine cane sugar and a special raising ingredient to guarantee you a gorgeous cake — or double your money back!

Golden! Light!

Scones more delicious than ever before with New Puffin Scone Mix!

Puffin Scone Mix

YOU MAKE TWO DOZEN GOLDEN, LIGHT SCONES

Just add milk to new Puffin Scone Mix — then mix and bake. Fifteen minutes later you're looking at the highest, lightest, most handsome scones you've ever baked! *No more weighing, sifting, measuring or rubbing in the shortening.*

All the work — gone forever! Puffin Scones are made with such little effort, you'll never stop being amazed.

Puffin Scone Mix makes many other delicious recipes, too. Pikelets, pancakes, rock cakes, savoury pinwheels and tea-cakes . . . they're but a few of the delicious variety of recipes you'll make so easily and quickly with Puffin Scone Mix. All the recipes are right on the Puffin packet.

Double-money-back guarantee
— so try Puffin soon as you like.

DATE SCONES WITH WHIPPED CARAMEL BUTTER

PREP + COOK TIME 40 MINUTES   MAKES 18

30g (1 ounce) butter, softened
¼ cup (55g) firmly packed light brown sugar
1 egg yolk
2½ cups (375g) self-raising flour
⅓ cup (50g) finely chopped seeded dried dates
1¼ cups (310ml) buttermilk

WHIPPED CARAMEL BUTTER
150g (5 ounces) unsalted butter, softened
¼ cup (55g) firmly packed light brown sugar
2 teaspoons vanilla extract

1 Preheat oven to 220°C/425°F. Grease 22cm (9-inch) square cake pan.

2 Beat butter, sugar and egg yolk in small bowl with electric mixer until light and fluffy. Transfer mixture to large bowl; add sifted flour, dates and buttermilk. Use a knife to cut the buttermilk through the flour mixture to make a soft, sticky dough. Turn dough onto floured surface, knead gently until smooth.

3 Press dough out to 20cm (8-inch) square, cut into nine squares, using a floured knife, then cut each square in half diagonally. Place scones side by side, just touching, in pan. Brush scones with a little extra buttermilk.

4 Bake scones about 20 minutes.

5 Meanwhile, make whipped caramel butter.

6 Serve warm scones with whipped caramel butter.

WHIPPED CARAMEL BUTTER Beat ingredients in small bowl with electric mixer until light and fluffy.

NUTRITIONAL COUNT PER SCONE 9.1g total fat (5.8g saturated); 790kJ (189 cal); 23.5g carbohydrate; 3.1g protein; 1.1g fibre

TIP Scones are best made on the day of serving. They can be frozen for up to 3 months. Thaw in oven, wrapped in foil.

LIMONCELLO MERINGUE PIES

PREP + COOK TIME 1 HOUR 15 MINUTES (+ REFRIGERATION & COOLING) MAKES 24

1¾ cups (260g) plain (all-purpose) flour
¼ cup (40g) icing (confectioners') sugar
185g (6 ounces) cold unsalted butter,
   chopped coarsely
1 egg yolk
2 teaspoons iced water, approximately
3 egg whites
¾ cup (165g) caster (superfine) sugar

LIMONCELLO CURD

3 egg yolks
½ cup (110g) caster (superfine) sugar
1 teaspoon finely grated lemon rind
¼ cup (60ml) lemon juice
90g (3 ounces) cold unsalted butter,
   chopped
1 tablespoon limoncello liqueur

1 Make limoncello curd.
2 Process flour, icing sugar and butter until crumbly. With motor operating, add egg yolk and enough of the water to make ingredients come together. Turn dough onto floured surface, knead gently until smooth. Wrap pastry in plastic; refrigerate 30 minutes.
3 Grease two 12-hole (1-tablespoon/20ml) mini muffin pans. Roll out half the pastry between sheets of baking paper until 5mm (¼-inch) thick. Cut out 12 x 6cm (2¼-inch) rounds; press rounds into holes of one pan. Prick base of cases well with a fork. Repeat with remaining pastry. Refrigerate 30 minutes.
4 Meanwhile, preheat oven to 220°C/425°F.
5 Bake cases about 12 minutes. Stand cases 5 minutes; transfer to wire rack to cool.
6 Beat egg whites in small bowl with electric mixer until soft peaks form. Gradually add caster sugar, beating until dissolved between additions.
7 Increase oven temperature to 240°C/475°F.
8 Divide limoncello curd into cases. Spoon meringue mixture into piping bag fitted with 1cm (½-inch) plain tube; pipe meringue over curd. Bake about 2 minutes. Cool.

LIMONCELLO CURD Whisk egg yolks and sugar in medium heatproof bowl until pale and thickened slightly. Whisk in rind and juice; stir over medium saucepan of simmering water about 12 minutes or until mixture coats the back of a spoon. Remove from heat; gradually whisk in butter until combined between additions. Stir in limoncello. Cover, refrigerate overnight.

NUTRITIONAL COUNT PER PIE 10.5g total fat (6.5g saturated fat); 623kJ (149 cal); 21.5g carbohydrate; 2.2g protein; 0.4g fibre

TIP Pastry cases and curd can be made 2 days ahead. Store the cases in an airtight container and the curd in the refrigerator.

RHUBARB FRANGIPANE TARTS

PREP + COOK TIME 1 HOUR 10 MINUTES (+ COOLING) MAKES 12

1 vanilla bean

½ cup (110g) caster (superfine) sugar

¼ cup (60ml) water

10 stalks trimmed rhubarb (300g), cut into
    4cm (1½-inch) lengths

40g (1½-inch) butter, softened

2 tablespoons caster (superfine) sugar, extra

½ teaspoon vanilla extract

1 egg yolk

½ cup (60g) ground almonds

2 teaspoons plain (all-purpose) flour

1 sheet butter puff pastry

1 Preheat oven to 180°C/350°F. Grease two oven trays.

2 Split vanilla bean, scrape seeds into small saucepan; discard pods.
Add sugar and the water to pan; stir syrup over heat, without boiling,
until sugar dissolves. Combine rhubarb and syrup in medium baking dish;
bake, uncovered, about 15 minutes or until rhubarb is tender. Cool.
Drain rhubarb; reserve syrup.

3 Meanwhile, beat butter, extra sugar, extract and egg yolk in small bowl
with electric mixer until light and fluffy. Stir in ground almonds and flour.

4 Cut pastry into quarters; cut each quarter into three rectangles. Place pastry
rectangles about 5cm (2 inches) apart on trays; spread rounded teaspoons
of almond mixture over each rectangle, leaving a 5mm (¼-inch) border. Top
with rhubarb; fold pastry edges in towards centre to form raised border.

5 Bake tarts about 25 minutes.

6 Serve tarts warm, brushed with reserved syrup.

NUTRITIONAL COUNT PER TART 9.2g total fat (3.9g saturated fat); 539kJ (129 cal);
18g carbohydrate; 2.5g protein; 1.2g fibre

6

The
SUPPER CLUB

SUPPER CLUBS FIRST APPEARED IN THE USA IN THE FORTIES: THESE ESTABLISHMENTS OFFERED FINE DINING, MUSIC AND A HIGH-CLASS IMAGE. BY THE FIFTIES, THEY HAD BECOME A HAVEN FOR SOCIAL NETWORKING AND, OF COURSE, THE DATING SCENE. SUPPER AFTER THE THEATRE OR THE 'PICTURES' WAS SERVED AT HOME, TOO, WITH THE SAME SWISH SILVERWARE, FINE CROCKERY AND GLASSWARE AND A MENU INCLUDING FINGER FOOD AND LUXURIOUS DESSERT CAKES.

SCOTCH EGGS WITH HERB MAYONNAISE

PREP + COOK TIME 55 MINUTES MAKES 6

7 eggs
1 tablespoon plain (all-purpose) flour
1 tablespoon milk
500g (1 pound) sausage mince
⅔ cup (70g) packaged breadcrumbs
vegetable oil, for deep-frying
HERB MAYONNAISE
½ cup (150g) mayonnaise
1 tablespoon lemon juice
1 tablespoon each finely chopped
    fresh chives and oregano

1 Boil six of the eggs in medium saucepan of water about 6 minutes or until hard. Cool, then peel.

2 Meanwhile, make herb mayonnaise.

3 Place flour in small shallow bowl. Beat remaining egg and milk in small bowl until combined. Toss hard-boiled eggs in flour; shake off excess. Divide sausage mince into six portions; using floured hands, shape mince around each egg. Dip in egg mixture, then in breadcrumbs.

4 Heat oil in wok or deep, wide saucepan; deep-fry eggs, in batches, until browned and cooked through. Drain on absorbent paper. Serve with herb mayonnaise.

HERB MAYONNAISE Combine ingredients in small bowl; season to taste.

NUTRITIONAL COUNT PER EGG 42.6g total fat (12.6g saturated fat); 2211kJ (529 cal); 16.6g carbohydrate; 19.7g protein; 2.2g fibre

CLASSIC RETRO RECIPE

CREPES SUZETTE

PREP + COOK TIME 1 HOUR 10 MINUTES (+ STANDING)   SERVES 4

¾ cup (110g) plain (all-purpose) flour
3 eggs
2 tablespoons vegetable oil
¾ cup (180ml) milk

ORANGE SAUCE

125g (4 ounces) unsalted butter
½ cup (110g) caster (superfine) sugar
1½ cups (375ml) orange juice
2 tablespoons lemon juice
⅓ cup (80ml) orange-flavoured liqueur

1 Sift flour into medium bowl, make well in centre; add eggs and oil then gradually whisk in milk until smooth. Pour batter into large jug, cover; stand 1 hour.

2 Heat greased heavy-based crêpe pan or small frying pan; pour ¼ cup of batter into pan, tilting pan to coat base. Cook, over low heat, until browned lightly, loosening edge of crêpe with spatula. Turn crêpe; brown other side. Remove crêpe from pan; cover to keep warm. Repeat with remaining batter to make a total of eight crêpes, greasing pan each time.

3 Make orange sauce.

4 Fold crêpes in half then in half again, place in sauce; warm over low heat.

5 Remove crêpes to serving plates; pour hot sauce over crêpes. Serve with orange slices, if you like.

ORANGE SAUCE Melt butter in large frying pan, add sugar; cook, stirring, until mixture begins to brown. Add strained juices; bring to the boil. Reduce heat; simmer, uncovered, about 3 minutes or until a golden colour. Remove from heat; add liqueur, ignite.

NUTRITIONAL COUNT PER SERVING 41g total fat (20.5g saturated fat); 3039kJ (727 cal); 66.9g carbohydrate; 10.3g protein; 1.3g fibre

TIPS Be very careful when igniting the sauce – use extra long matches, available from supermarkets or camping stores and make sure overhead exhaust fans are turned off. Igniting the sauce burns off the alcohol, leaving a more intense flavour. If you prefer, the sauce can be served as is, without first igniting it.

CLUB SANDWICH

HAM, EGG AND CHEESE TOASTIE

PREP + COOK TIME 20 MINUTES   MAKES 4

Cook 4 halved, rindless bacon slices in heated oiled large frying pan until crisp. Thinly slice 3 small tomatoes. Mash 1 medium avocado and 2 teaspoons lime juice in small bowl until smooth; season to taste. Spread ½ cup mayonnaise over 12 slices white bread. Top four slices with half the avocado mixture; top each slice with a large butter (boston) lettuce leaf. Top with half the tomato, half the bacon and 75g (2½ ounces) shaved turkey breast. Top with four more bread slices, mayonnaise-side down; spread top with a little more mayonnaise. Repeat with remaining avocado mixture, another four lettuce leaves, remaining tomato, remaining bacon, another 75g (2½ ounces) shaved turkey breast and bread slices. Cut into triangles; hold layers in place with toothpicks or skewers.

NUTRITIONAL COUNT PER SANDWICH 36.1g total fat (7.7g saturated fat); 3210kJ (768 cal); 69.9g carbohydrate; 37.7g protein; 6.3g fibre

PREP + COOK TIME 20 MINUTES   MAKES 1

Boil 1 egg in saucepan of water about 6 minutes or until hard. Cool, then peel and slice thinly. Spread 2 slices wholemeal bread with 1 tablespoon barbecue sauce; sandwich 30g (1 ounce) shaved ham, sliced egg and ¼ cup coarsely grated reduced-fat cheddar cheese between bread slices. Toast in sandwich press until golden brown.

NUTRITIONAL COUNT PER SANDWICH
16.1g total fat (6.9g saturated fat); 1898kJ (454 cal); 44.3g carbohydrate; 29.7g protein; 5.9g fibre

CHIPOLATA AND SWEET CHILLI SAUCE ROLLS

PRAWN SANDWICHES

PREP + COOK TIME 20 MINUTES   MAKES 8

Cook 8 lean beef chipolata sausages in heated oiled medium frying pan until browned and cooked through. Split 8 mini oval dinner rolls; spread with ¼ cup sweet chilli sauce. Fill rolls with 20g (¾ ounce) rocket (arugula) leaves, ¾ cup coarsely grated cheddar cheese and sausages.

NUTRITIONAL COUNT PER ROLL

12.3g total fat (6g saturated fat); 1037kJ (248 cal); 23.3g carbohydrate; 9.8g protein; 2.5g fibre

TIP This recipe is a great way to use up leftover sausages; sausages can be served hot or cold.

PREP TIME 30 MINUTES   MAKES 24

Shell and devein 12 cooked medium king prawns; slice in half lengthways. Combine ½ cup mayonnaise, 1 teaspoon finely grated lemon rind and 1 tablespoon lemon juice in small bowl; season to taste. Remove and discard crusts from 12 slices white bread; cut each slice in half diagonally. Spread each bread triangle with 1 teaspoon mayonnaise mixture; divide 50g (1½ ounces) baby rocket (arugula) leaves between triangles. Place one prawn half on top of each triangle. Fold triangles in half, bringing the two longest points together; secure with toothpicks.

NUTRITIONAL COUNT PER SANDWICH

2.5g total fat (0.3g saturated fat); 305kJ (73 cal); 8.4g carbohydrate; 3.8g protein; 0.5g fibre

CHEESY OMELETTES

PREP + COOK TIME 15 MINUTES MAKES 2

4 eggs
2 tablespoons water
10g (½ ounce) butter
⅓ cup (40g) coarsely grated cheddar cheese

1 Beat eggs and the water with a fork in medium jug.
Heat half the butter in small frying pan, add half the
egg mixture; tilt pan to cover base with egg mixture.
Cook over medium heat until omelette is almost set.
2 Sprinkle half the cheese over omelette; fold omelette
in half. Slide omelette onto plate; cover to keep warm.
Repeat with remaining butter, egg mixture and cheese
to make another omelette.
NUTRITIONAL COUNT PER OMELETTE 22.8g total fat
(10.7g saturated fat); 1191kJ (285 cal); 0.4g carbohydrate;
20.2g protein; 0g fibre
TIPS You need a frying pan with a 20cm (8-inch) base.
Add finely chopped fresh parsley or chives to the egg
mixture before cooking.

BLUE CHEESE AND FIG BITES

PREP + COOK TIME 20 **MINUTES** MAKES 12

⅓ cup roasted slivered almonds
2 green onions (scallions), chopped coarsely
1 cup loosely packed fresh mint leaves
⅓ cup (80ml) olive oil • 1 tablespoon lemon juice
1 loaf turkish bread (430g)
200g (6½ ounces) thinly sliced semi-dried figs
100g (3 ounces) blue cheese, sliced thinly

1 Blend or process almonds, onion, mint, oil and juice until smooth;
season to taste.
2 Preheat grill (broiler).
3 Halve bread loaf lengthways; cut each half lengthways into
three fingers then cut fingers into four crossways to get 24 slices.
Toast bread under grill.
4 Spread almond mixture on half the toasts; top with figs and cheese.
Top with remaining toast; serve warm.
NUTRITIONAL COUNT PER BITE 11.9g total fat (2.9g saturated fat);
1012kJ (242 cal); 25.5g carbohydrate; 6.2g protein; 3.9g fibre

CARAMELISED TOMATO AND HAM BITES

PREP + COOK TIME 40 **MINUTES** MAKES 16

2 shallots (50g), chopped finely
250g (8 ounces) cherry tomatoes, halved
¼ cup (60ml) balsamic vinegar
1 tablespoon light brown sugar • 1 loaf brioche (500g)
2 cups (240g) finely grated semi-hard sheep-milk cheese
185g (6 ounces) thinly sliced double smoked leg ham

1 Cook shallots in heated oiled medium frying pan until soft.
Add tomato; cook , stirring, 5 minutes. Add vinegar and sugar;
cook, stirring occasionally, until thickened. Season to taste.
2 Preheat grill (broiler).
3 Cut brioche loaf into 16 slices; cut 32 x 6.5cm (2¾-inch) rounds
from slices. Top half the slices with cheese; grill until cheese melts.
Toast remaining rounds until golden.
4 Top cheese toasts with ham; top with caramelised tomatoes then
remaining toasts. Serve warm.
NUTRITIONAL COUNT PER BITE 7.5g total fat (4.1g saturated fat);
644kJ (154 cal); 12.7g carbohydrate; 8.4g protein; 0.7g fibre

Save Money!

This bottle makes more than **2 dozen brimming glasses** of Mynor Fruit Cup!

..it costs you *less than* **2d. a glass**

MADE FROM ORANGES AND BLENDED FRUITS

EXPORT QUALITY

MYNOR FRUIT CUP

FRUIT JUICE CORDIAL

MYNOR MEANS FRUIT JUICE

MOTHERS! Here's the most healthy drink you can give those thirsty children of yours! Pure, delicious Mynor, rich in all those essential vitamins A, B, C and D contained in the fresh juices of oranges, lemons, pineapples and passionfruit. And, just imagine what these would cost you to buy at present-day prices! Pour a little Mynor Fruit Cup into a glass, fill it with pure, wholesome water, and let the children drink as much as they want. Just think . . . all this costs *less than* 2d. a glass!

MYNOR FRUIT CUP

P.S.: 2d. refund on undamaged Mynor bottles returned to your supplier in Sydney metropolitan area.

MEDALLION

MEDALLION 5 Way TOPPING CHOCOLATE

Summertime Hit

5 WAY TOPPING LIFTS EVERY DESSERT

IN ALL FLAVOURS

STRAWBERRY

PINEAPPLE

RASPBERRY

PASSIONFRUIT

LIME

Use Medallion Topping 5 ways—

1. Ice cream topping.　2. Milk drinks.

3. Milk and ice blocks.　4. Cake icing and filling.　5. As a flavour.

Ask your grocer!

Here's another cool treat — Medallion Fruit Juice Cordials

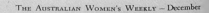

COFFEE HAZELNUT MERINGUES

PREP + COOK TIME 1 HOUR (+ COOLING)   MAKES 30

2 egg whites • ½ cup (110g) caster (superfine) sugar
2 teaspoons instant coffee granules
½ teaspoon hot water
3 teaspoons coffee-flavoured liqueur
¼ cup (35g) roasted hazelnuts

1 Preheat oven to 120°C/250°F. Grease oven trays; line with baking paper.
2 Beat egg whites in small bowl with electric mixer until soft peaks form; gradually add sugar, beating until sugar dissolves.
3 Meanwhile, dissolve coffee in the water in small jug; stir in liqueur. Fold coffee mixture into meringue mixture.
4 Spoon mixture into piping bag fitted with 5mm (¼-inch) fluted tube. Pipe meringues onto trays 2cm (¾ inch) apart; top each meringue with a nut.
5 Bake meringues about 45 minutes. Cool in oven with door ajar.
NUTRITIONAL COUNT PER MERINGUE 0.7g total fat (0g saturated fat); 46kJ (11 cal); 4g carbohydrate; 0.6g protein; 0.1g fibre

RUM AND RAISIN CHOCOLATE SLICE

PREP + COOK TIME 35 MINUTES (+ STANDING & REFRIGERATION)   MAKES 12

½ cup (75g) chopped raisins • 2 tablespoons dark rum, warmed
150g (4½ ounces) milk eating chocolate, chopped
2 teaspoons vegetable oil • ¼ cup (60ml) pouring cream
200g (6½ ounces) dark eating (semi-sweet) chocolate, chopped

1 Combine raisins and rum in small bowl. Cover; stand 3 hours.
2 Grease 8cm x 25cm (3¼-inch x 10-inch) bar cake pan; line base and two long sides with foil, extending foil 5cm (2 inches) over long sides.
3 Stir half the milk chocolate and half the oil in small heatproof bowl over small saucepan of simmering water until smooth; spread mixture over base of pan. Refrigerate 10 minutes or until set.
4 Stir cream and dark chocolate in small saucepan over low heat until smooth. Stir in raisin mixture, spread over chocolate base; refrigerate 20 minutes or until set.
5 Stir remaining milk chocolate and oil in small heatproof bowl over small saucepan of simmering water until smooth; spread over raisin mixture. Refrigerate about 40 minutes or until set.
NUTRITIONAL COUNT PER PIECE 11.2g total fat (6.5g saturated fat); 849kJ (203 cal); 22.8g carbohydrate; 2.1g protein; 0.6g fibre

Original recipes and photographs from the iconic *The Australian Women's Weekly Cookery In Colour*, published in 1960 by *The Australian Women's Weekly* in conjunction with Paul Hamlyn, London.

PINK VELVET CAKE

PREP + COOK TIME 1 HOUR (+ COOLING & FREEZING) SERVES 12

125g (4 ounces) butter, softened

1 teaspoon vanilla extract

1½ cups (330g) caster (superfine) sugar

2 eggs

1½ cups (225g) plain (all-purpose) flour

2 tablespoons cornflour (cornstarch)

2 tablespoons cocoa powder

1 cup (250ml) buttermilk

1 tablespoon rose pink food colouring

1 teaspoon white vinegar

1 teaspoon bicarbonate of soda (baking soda)

1 cup (50g) flaked coconut

MASCARPONE FROSTING

250g (8 ounces) cream cheese, softened

250g (8 ounces) mascarpone cheese

1 cup (160g) icing (confectioners') sugar

1 teaspoon vanilla extract

1¼ cups (310ml) thickened (heavy) cream

1 Preheat oven to 180°C/350°F. Grease two deep 22cm (9-inch) round cake pans; line bases and sides with baking paper.

2 Beat butter, extract, sugar and eggs in small bowl with electric mixer until light and fluffy. Transfer mixture to large bowl; stir in sifted flours and cocoa and combined buttermilk and food colouring, in two batches.

3 Combine vinegar and soda in a cup; allow to fizz then fold into cake mixture. Divide mixture between pans.

4 Bake cakes about 25 minutes. Stand cakes 10 minutes before turning top-side up onto wire rack to cool. Wrap cakes in plastic; freeze 40 minutes.

5 Meanwhile, make mascarpone frosting.

6 Split cold cakes in half. Place one layer on serving plate, cut-side up; spread with ⅔ cup frosting. Repeat layering, finishing with remaining frosting spread over top and side of cake; press coconut onto side of cake.

MASCARPONE FROSTING Beat cream cheese, mascarpone, sugar and extract in small bowl with electric mixer until smooth. Beat in cream.

NUTRITIONAL COUNT PER SERVING 41.4g total fat (27.1g saturated fat); 2165kJ (518 cal); 59.4g carbohydrate; 7.2g protein; 1.4g fibre

TIPS It is fine to use just one 300ml carton of cream for this recipe. To make your own buttermilk equivalent, combine 1 tablespoon fresh lemon juice with enough reduced-fat milk to make 1 cup. Stand a few minutes until thickened then stir.

ORANGE ALMOND VICTORIA SPONGE

PREP + COOK TIME 55 MINUTES (+ COOLING) SERVES 12

185g (6 ounces) unsalted butter, softened

1 teaspoon vanilla extract

¾ cup (165g) caster (superfine) sugar

3 eggs

¼ cup (60ml) milk

1½ cups (225g) self-raising flour

1 cup (320g) orange marmalade, warmed

1¼ cups (310ml) thickened (heavy) cream

2 tablespoons icing (confectioners') sugar

½ cup (40g) flaked almonds, roasted

1 Preheat oven to 180°C/350°F. Grease deep 20cm (8-inch) ring pan well with butter.

2 Beat butter, extract and caster sugar in small bowl with electric mixer until light and fluffy. Beat in eggs, one at a time. Stir in milk and sifted flour, in two batches. Spread mixture into pan.

3 Bake cake about 30 minutes. Turn sponge immediately onto baking-paper-covered wire rack, turn top-side up to cool.

4 Meanwhile, strain marmalade through fine sieve; reserve syrup and rind separately.

5 Beat cream and half the icing sugar in small bowl with electric mixer until soft peaks form.

6 Split sponge into three layers. Place one layer onto serving plate, cut-side up; spread with half of the marmalade syrup. Top with another layer of sponge and remaining syrup; top with remaining layer of sponge. Cut sponge into twelve pieces, keeping cake in ring shape.

7 Spread two-thirds of the cream around side of sponge; press almonds onto cream. Spoon remaining cream into piping bag fitted with 1cm (½-inch) fluted tube. Pipe rosettes on top of cake; top with some of the reserved rind. Serve sponge dusted with remaining icing sugar.

NUTRITIONAL COUNT PER SERVING 25.8g total fat (15.3g saturated fat); 1601kJ (383 cal); 47.6g carbohydrate; 5g protein; 1.2g fibre

TIP It is fine to use just one 300ml carton of cream for this recipe.

BLACK FOREST GATEAUX

PREP + COOK TIME 1 HOUR 15 MINUTES (+ COOLING) MAKES 40

185g (6 ounces) unsalted butter, softened
1½ cups (330g) caster (superfine) sugar
6 eggs, separated
¾ cup (110g) self-raising flour
⅔ cup (70g) cocoa powder
2 tablespoons milk
½ cup (125ml) blackcurrant liqueur or
   cherry brandy
1 cup (320g) black cherry jam
1¼ cups (310ml) thickened (heavy)
   cream, whipped
1 cup (200g) drained, seeded sour
   cherries, halved

CHOCOLATE GANACHE

½ cup (125ml) pouring cream
220g (7 ounces) dark eating (semi-sweet)
   chocolate, chopped coarsely

1 Preheat oven to 180°C/350°F. Grease 20cm x 30cm (8-inch x 12-inch) lamington pan; line with baking paper, extending paper 5cm (2 inches) over long sides.
2 Beat butter, sugar and egg yolks in small bowl with electric mixer until light and fluffy. Stir in sifted flour and cocoa and milk, in two batches.
3 Beat egg whites in small bowl with electric mixer until soft peaks form. Fold egg whites into cake mixture, in two batches. Spread mixture into pan.
4 Bake cake about 35 minutes. Stand cake 5 minutes before turning, top-side up, onto wire rack to cool.
5 Meanwhile, make chocolate ganache.
6 Trim edges from all sides of cake; cut cake into 40 squares. Split each square in half; brush each half with liqueur. Sandwich cakes with jam and cream; top with chocolate ganache and cherries.

CHOCOLATE GANACHE Bring cream to the boil in small saucepan. Remove from heat; pour over chocolate in small bowl, stir until smooth. Stand at room temperature until thickened slightly.

NUTRITIONAL COUNT PER SERVING 10.8g total fat (7.2g saturated fat); 694kJ (166 cal); 21.8g carbohydrate; 2.2g protein; 0.6g fibre

TIP It is fine to use just one 300ml carton of cream for this recipe.

7

Simple FAMILY FOOD

WITH A FEW EXCEPTIONS, EVERYONE ATE AT HOME
FIFTY YEARS AGO AND THE HOUSEWIVES OF THE DAY
WORKED TIRELESSLY PREPARING BREAKFAST, LUNCH
AND DINNER, AND AFTERNOON TEAS AND SUPPER.
FAMILY FOOD WAS HEARTY AND SIMPLE, AND SERVINGS
WERE GENEROUS. MEAT WAS SUPPLEMENTED BY
PRODUCE FROM THE KITCHEN GARDEN BUT, AS THE
CENTURY WORE ON, FROZEN VEGETABLES AND
TINNED GOODS BEGAN TO MAKE AN APPEARANCE.

CORNED BEEF WITH PARSLEY SAUCE

PREP + COOK TIME 2 HOURS 10 MINUTES (+ COOLING & STANDING) SERVES 4

1.5kg (3-pound) piece beef
   corned silverside
2 dried bay leaves
6 black peppercorns
1 large brown onion (200g), quartered
1 large carrot (180g), chopped coarsely
1 tablespoon brown malt vinegar
¼ cup (50g) firmly packed light
   brown sugar

PARSLEY SAUCE
30g (1 ounce) butter
¼ cup (35g) plain (all-purpose) flour
2½ cups (625ml) milk
⅓ cup (40g) coarsely grated cheddar cheese
⅓ cup finely chopped fresh flat-leaf parsley
1 tablespoon mild mustard

1 Place beef, bay leaves, peppercorns, onion, carrot, vinegar and half the sugar in large saucepan. Add enough water to just cover beef; simmer, covered, about 2 hours or until beef is tender. Cool beef 1 hour in liquid in pan.

2 Remove beef from pan; discard liquid. Sprinkle sheet of foil with remaining sugar, wrap beef in foil; stand 20 minutes then slice thinly.

3 Meanwhile, make parsley sauce.

4 Serve sliced corned beef with parsley sauce.

PARSLEY SAUCE Heat butter in small saucepan, add flour; cook, stirring, until mixture thickens and bubbles. Gradually stir in milk; cook, stirring, until sauce boils and thickens. Remove from heat; stir in cheese, parsley and mustard. Season to taste.

NUTRITIONAL COUNT PER SERVING 35.8g total fat (19.3g saturated fat); 3520kJ (842 cal); 31g carbohydrate; 97g protein; 2.5g fibre

SERVING SUGGESTION Serve with roasted potatoes and steamed green beans.

CLASSIC RETRO RECIPE

SHEPHERD'S PIE

PREP + COOK TIME 1 HOUR SERVES 4

30g (1 ounce) butter

1 medium brown onion (150g),
  chopped finely

1 medium carrot (120g), chopped finely

½ teaspoon dried mixed herbs

4 cups (750g) finely chopped cooked lamb

¼ cup (70g) tomato paste

¼ cup (60ml) tomato sauce (ketchup)

2 tablespoons worcestershire sauce

2 cups (500ml) beef stock

2 tablespoons plain (all-purpose) flour

⅓ cup (80ml) water

POTATO TOPPING

5 medium potatoes (1kg), chopped coarsely

60g (2 ounces) butter, chopped coarsely

¼ cup (60ml) milk

1 Preheat oven to 200°C/400°F. Oil deep 2.5-litre (10-cup) ovenproof dish.

2 Make potato topping.

3 Heat butter in large saucepan; cook onion and carrot, stirring, until vegetables are tender. Add mixed herbs and lamb; cook, stirring, 2 minutes. Stir in paste, sauces and stock, then blended flour and the water; cook, stirring, until mixture boils and thickens. Season. Pour mixture into dish.

4 Spoon potato topping into piping bag fitted with a large fluted nozzle; pipe over lamb mixture.

5 Bake pie 20 minutes or until browned lightly.

POTATO TOPPING Boil, steam or microwave potato until tender; drain. Mash potato in medium bowl with butter and milk until smooth; season to taste.

NUTRITIONAL COUNT PER SERVING 36.2g total fat (20.2g saturated fat); 2976kJ (712 cal); 44.7g carbohydrate; 48.8g protein; 6.6g fibre

SALMON PATTIES
WITH DILL CREAM SAUCE

PREP + COOK TIME 50 MINUTES (+ REFRIGERATION)   SERVES 4

4 medium potatoes (800g), chopped coarsely

40g (1½ ounces) butter, softened

1 egg

½ cup (40g) finely grated parmesan cheese

415g (13 ounces) canned pink salmon,
   drained, flaked

4 green onions (scallions), sliced thinly

1 clove garlic, crushed

½ cup (50g) packaged breadcrumbs

vegetable oil, for shallow-frying

200g (6½ ounces) green beans, trimmed

DILL CREAM SAUCE

⅓ cup (80ml) dry white wine

1¼ cups (310ml) pouring cream

1 tablespoon horseradish cream

2 teaspoons lemon juice

1 tablespoon finely chopped fresh dill

1 Boil, steam or microwave potato until tender; drain. Mash potato in large bowl with butter, egg and cheese until smooth.

2 Drain salmon; discard skin and bones. Add salmon, onion and garlic to potato mixture, season; mix well. Shape salmon mixture into eight patties; coat in breadcrumbs. Place patties on tray. Cover; refrigerate 30 minutes.

3 Heat oil in large frying pan; shallow-fry patties, in batches, until browned lightly and heated through. Drain on absorbent paper.

4 Meanwhile, make dill cream sauce.

5 Boil, steam or microwave beans until tender; drain.

6 Serve patties with beans and dill cream sauce.

DILL CREAM SAUCE Bring wine to the boil in small saucepan; boil, uncovered, until reduced by half. Add cream, horseradish cream and juice; cook, stirring, about 3 minutes or until sauce thickens slightly. Stir in dill; season to taste.

NUTRITIONAL COUNT PER SERVING 79.6g total fat (34.8g saturated fat); 4272kJ (1022 cal); 39.3g carbohydrate; 33.4g protein; 5.5g fibre

TIP It is fine to use just one 300ml carton of cream for this recipe.

TURKEY AND CRANBERRY MEATLOAF

PREP + COOK TIME 1 HOUR 20 MINUTES   SERVES 4

10 slices prosciutto (150g)
1 medium brown onion (150g), grated coarsely
2 green onions (scallions), sliced thinly
2 cloves garlic, crushed
750g (1½ pounds) minced (ground) turkey
2 tablespoons tomato sauce (ketchup)
1 tablespoon worcestershire sauce
1 egg yolk
½ cup (35g) stale breadcrumbs
⅓ cup finely chopped fresh flat-leaf parsley
½ cup (160g) cranberry sauce
2 tablespoons orange juice

1 Preheat oven to 200°C/400°F.
2 Oil 15cm x 20cm (6-inch x 8-inch) loaf pan. Line base and sides of pan with prosciutto, slightly overlapping the slices and allowing overhang on long sides of pan.
3 Combine onions, garlic, turkey, sauces, egg yolk, breadcrumbs and parsley in large bowl; season. Press into pan. Fold prosciutto over to cover turkey mixture. Place pan on oven tray. Bake 45 minutes.
4 Meanwhile, combine cranberry sauce and juice in small bowl.
5 Remove meatloaf from oven; drain juices from pan. Carefully invert meatloaf onto wire rack. Place rack over oven tray. Brush meatloaf with cranberry mixture; return to oven, bake about 15 minutes or until browned and cooked through.
NUTRITIONAL COUNT PER SERVING 12.2g total fat (3.4g saturated fat); 1760kJ (421 cal); 28.8g carbohydrate; 47.7g protein; 1.7g fibre

SPICY CHICKEN TACOS

PREP + COOK TIME 25 MINUTES MAKES 10

1 tablespoon olive oil • 1 medium brown onion (150g), chopped
500g (1 pound) minced (ground) chicken
35g (1-ounce) packet taco seasoning mix
375g (12 ounces) bottled thick and chunky taco sauce
½ cup (125ml) water • 10 stand 'n' stuff taco shells (140g)
1 cup finely shredded iceberg lettuce
1 medium carrot (120g), grated coarsely
125g (4 ounces) cherry tomatoes, quartered
½ cup (60g) coarsely grated cheddar cheese
½ cup loosely packed fresh coriander (cilantro) leaves
⅓ cup (80g) sour cream

1 Heat oil in large frying pan; cook onion, stirring, until softened.
Add chicken; cook, stirring, until browned. Add taco seasoning;
cook, stirring, until fragrant. Add half the taco sauce and the water;
cook, stirring, about 7 minutes or until mixture thickens. Season.
2 Meanwhile, heat taco shells according to directions on packet.
3 Spoon chicken mixture into shells; top with lettuce, carrot, tomato,
cheese, coriander and remaining sauce. Serve topped with sour cream.
NUTRITIONAL COUNT PER TACO 35.9g total fat (13.3g saturated fat);
2445kJ (585 cal); 29.7g carbohydrate; 33.2g protein; 6.7g fibre

LAMB SHANK AND VEGETABLE SOUP

PREP + COOK TIME 2 HOURS SERVES 4

4 lamb shanks (1kg)
2 medium carrots (240g), chopped coarsely
2 medium white onions (300g), chopped coarsely
2 cloves garlic, crushed
2 medium potatoes (400g), chopped coarsely
2 stalks celery (300g), trimmed, chopped coarsely
400g (12½ ounces) canned chopped tomatoes
1.5 litres (6 cups) beef or chicken stock
½ cup (140g) tomato paste
2 medium zucchini (240g), chopped coarsely

1 Place shanks, carrot, onion, garlic, potato, celery, undrained
tomatoes, stock and paste in large saucepan; bring to the boil.
Reduce heat; simmer, covered, 1 hour.
2 Add zucchini; simmer, uncovered, 30 minutes or until shanks are tender.
3 Remove shanks from soup. When cool enough to handle, remove
meat from bones, discard bones. Return meat to soup; stir until hot.
Season to taste.
NUTRITIONAL COUNT PER SERVING 9.2g total fat (3.9g saturated fat);
1513kJ (362 cal); 29.2g carbohydrate; 39.7g protein; 8.5g fibre

Just five simple ingredients
and *Leggo's Tomato Paste*

...makes the astiest Spaghetti* is side of Napoli

never a recipe says "tomatoes", then u need Leggo's Tomato Paste — a e times concentrate of the pick of ing, sun ripe tomatoes. Ready to use smooth, no messy skin or seeds, and to blend into whatever dish you're king. A small 5-oz. tin equals 2 lbs. of tomatoes. Use it to add richer, r flavour to soups, sauces, casseroles; d for some real cooking fun, try tinental dishes using Leggo's Tomato , like the easy to prepare, easy-on- e-pocket Spaghetti Marinara here . . .

paghetti Marinara *

t cook your spaghetti in boiling water (about minutes). When cooked, wash immediately a colander under running water. Strain, heat ain, and place in warm shallow dish.

UCE: Cut 1 clove of garlic and 1 onion very ly and fry in cooking oil. Add 1 small tin dines and cook all together for 3 or 4 minutes. solve 3 teaspoons of Leggo's Tomato Paste ½ cup of water. Salt and pepper to taste. d to other ingredients, bring all to boil and mer 4 to 5 minutes. If necessary, extra cook- oil may be added when cooked. Pour over ghetti and serve.

Leggo's
make meals *magic!*

For cheerier eating — choose from the good things in Leggo's Pantry. Tomato Sauce, Savory Relish, Pickles, Spaghetti Sauce, Tomato Juice, Soup.

Made at the new modern factory of—
H. M. LEGGO & CO. LTD., OAK AVENUE, MENTONE. TELEPHONE XB 1266

TRIPLO CONCENTRATO DI POMODORO
Leggo's
TOMATO PASTE

BAKED ASPARAGUS RISOTTO

PREP + COOK TIME 1 HOUR 10 MINUTES   SERVES 4

3½ cups (875ml) chicken or vegetable stock

2 teaspoons finely grated lemon rind

¼ cup (60ml) lemon juice

1 tablespoon olive oil

1 medium brown onion (150g), chopped finely

1 clove garlic, crushed

1½ cups (300g) arborio rice

170g (5½ ounces) asparagus, trimmed,
   cut into 2.5cm (1-inch) lengths

250g (8 ounces) cherry tomatoes, halved

⅓ cup (25g) finely grated parmesan cheese

2 teaspoons finely chopped fresh thyme

1 Preheat oven to 180°C/350°F.

2 Bring stock, rind and juice to the boil in medium saucepan. Reduce heat; simmer, covered.

3 Meanwhile, heat oil in medium saucepan; cook onion and garlic, stirring, until onion softens. Add rice; stir to coat in onion mixture. Stir in simmering stock mixture. Transfer mixture to shallow large ovenproof dish; cover with foil.

4 Bake risotto 25 minutes, stirring halfway through cooking. Add asparagus and tomato; bake, uncovered, about 25 minutes or until rice is tender. Season.

5 Remove risotto from oven; sprinkle with cheese and thyme.

NUTRITIONAL COUNT PER SERVING 8g total fat (2.5g saturated fat); 1262kJ (388 cal); 65.2g carbohydrate; 11.5g protein; 2.7g fibre

TIP Baked risotto is a delicious alternative to the usual hand-stirred risotto (and a lot easier, too). Be sure to cover the risotto mixture tightly with foil while baking to ensure a perfectly creamy result.

CHICKEN, LEEK AND MUSHROOM PIES

PREP + COOK TIME **1 HOUR** SERVES 4

1 tablespoon vegetable oil
1 medium leek (350g), sliced thinly
2 rindless bacon slices (130g), sliced thinly
200g (6½ ounces) button mushrooms, halved
1 tablespoon plain (all-purpose) flour
1 cup (250ml) chicken stock
⅓ cup (80ml) pouring cream
1 tablespoon dijon mustard
3 cups (480g) coarsely chopped barbecued chicken
1 sheet puff pastry, quartered

1 Preheat oven to 200°C/400°F.
2 Heat oil in medium saucepan; cook leek, bacon and mushrooms, stirring, until leek softens. Stir in flour; cook, stirring, until mixture thickens and bubbles. Gradually add stock; cook, stirring, until mixture boils and thickens. Stir in cream, mustard and chicken. Season to taste.
3 Divide mixture into four 1-cup (250ml) ovenproof dishes; top each with a pastry quarter, press around edges to seal.
4 Bake pies about 20 minutes or until browned.
NUTRITIONAL COUNT PER SERVING 44.7g total fat (13.1g saturated fat); 2780kJ (665 cal); 20.4g carbohydrate; 44.5g protein; 3.7g fibre
TIP You need to purchase a large barbecued chicken weighing about 900g (1¾ pounds) for this recipe.

MIXED MUSHROOM STROGANOFF

PREP + COOK TIME 40 MINUTES   SERVES 4

375g (12 ounces) fettuccine pasta

1 tablespoon olive oil

20g (¾ ounce) butter

3 shallots (75g), sliced thinly

2 cloves garlic, sliced thinly

3 teaspoons smoked paprika

2 tablespoons dijon mustard

350g (11 ounces) button mushrooms, sliced thinly

200g (6½ ounces) swiss brown mushrooms, sliced thinly

200g (6½ ounces) fresh shiitake mushrooms, sliced thinly

¼ cup (60ml) dry white wine

¾ cup (180ml) vegetable stock

1 cup (240g) sour cream

1 Cook pasta in large saucepan of boiling water until tender; drain. Rinse under cold water; drain.

2 Meanwhile, heat oil and half the butter in large saucepan; cook shallot and garlic, stirring, until shallot softens. Add paprika and mustard; cook, stirring, 1 minute. Stir in mushrooms and remaining butter. Cover; cook 10 minutes, stirring occasionally. Add wine and stock; cook, uncovered, about 5 minutes or until liquid is reduced slightly. Add sour cream; simmer gently, uncovered, 5 minutes. Season to taste.

3 Serve stroganoff over pasta.

NUTRITIONAL COUNT PER SERVING 34.4g total fat (19.3g saturated fat); 2863kJ (685 cal); 68.7g carbohydrate; 18.8g protein; 8.3g fibre

TIPS If you have some lean beef in the freezer, substitute half the mushrooms for the sliced beef, browning the beef in oil and returning it to the pan just before serving. You can stir ¼ cup coarsely chopped fresh flat-leaf parsley into the stroganoff just before serving.

TIP YOU COULD USE THE SAME AMOUNT OF PUMPKIN IN THIS RECIPE INSTEAD OF KUMARA IF YOU LIKE.

BAKED PENNE WITH KUMARA AND SPINACH

PREP + COOK TIME 1 HOUR 10 MINUTES   SERVES 6

2 medium red onions (340g), cut into wedges
600g (1¼ pounds) kumara (orange sweet potato),
   sliced thickly
2 tablespoons olive oil
375g (12 ounces) penne pasta
250g (8 ounces) frozen spinach, thawed, drained
1½ cups (360g) ricotta cheese
1 clove garlic, crushed
¼ cup (60ml) pouring cream
800g (1½ pounds) canned crushed tomatoes
¼ cup (40g) pine nuts
½ cup (40g) finely grated parmesan cheese

1 Preheat oven to 220°C/425°F.
2 Combine onion and kumara with oil in large baking dish;
roast, uncovered, stirring once, about 40 minutes or until tender.
3 Meanwhile, cook pasta in large saucepan of boiling water
until tender; drain.
4 Combine pasta, spinach, ricotta, garlic, cream and tomatoes
in large bowl; season to taste.
5 Spread kumara mixture over base of 3-litre (12-cup) baking
dish. Top with pasta mixture; sprinkle with nuts and parmesan.
6 Bake, covered, 10 minutes. Uncover; bake about 5 minutes or
until browned lightly.
NUTRITIONAL COUNT PER SERVING 25.3g total fat (9.8g saturated fat);
2450kJ (586 cal); 63.4g carbohydrate; 21.9g protein; 8.4g fibre

Simple Family Food

PR... ...KING

The colour ... ...me idea of the scope of cooking in ... ...ll find detailed instructions in your ... recipe book, but I have selected in this section some of the recit... ...d types of cooking which save you time and very often produce b... ...results than when cooked by ordinary methods.

882

SOUPS

Undoubtedly a pressure cooker is quite wonderful for stock and soups. You retain all the flavour of the ingredients, and the soup is cooked in a very short time. If adapting ordinary recipes there is almost no loss of liquid by evaporation, so in an ordinary recipe use considerably less (approximately half).

FISH

While fish is fairly quick-cooking under normal conditions it is even quicker in a pressure cooker. You keep a very good flavour and avoid the smell of fish in your kitchen. You can also put fish in the cooker with any vegetables you may wish, without there being any intermingling of flavours.

MEAT

A few recipes are included. For stews the saving of time is enormous. As with soup you must cut down the amount of liquid in an ordinary recipe. Meat such as tongue and ham which normally takes so long to cook is ready in a short time and wonderfully tender.

PUDDINGS

A variety of puddings can be cooked ... Egg custards don't curdle, steamed pu... in a much shorter time and it is qui... a creamy rice pudding.

VEGETABL...

Possibly one of the most popular ... cooker is for vegetables. It has be... correctly cooked in a pressure co... often even more, vitamins than ... means. To keep green vegetable... water in pressure cooker. Root... made exceptionally tender, an...

JAMS, BOTT...

A section has been devoted ... much saving of time with fr... ing the fruit for jam. Vege... only be done with a pressu...

Original recipes and photographs from the iconic *The Australian Women's Weekly Cookery In Colour*, published in 1960 by *The Australian Women's Weekly* in conjunction with Paul Hamlyn, London.

PASTITSIO

PREP + COOK TIME **2 HOURS 15 MINUTES**   SERVES **6**

250g (8 ounces) macaroni pasta

2 eggs, beaten lightly

¾ cup (60g) coarsely grated parmesan cheese

2 tablespoons stale breadcrumbs

MEAT SAUCE

2 tablespoons olive oil

2 medium brown onions (300g), chopped finely

750g (1½ pounds) minced (ground) beef

400g (12½ ounces) canned crushed tomatoes

⅓ cup (90g) tomato paste

½ cup (125ml) beef stock

¼ cup (60ml) dry white wine

½ teaspoon ground cinnamon

1 egg, beaten lightly

CHEESE TOPPING

90g (3 ounces) butter

½ cup (75g) plain (all-purpose) flour

3½ cups (875ml) milk

1 cup (80g) coarsely grated parmesan cheese

2 egg yolks

1 Preheat oven to 180°C/350°F. Oil shallow 2.5-litre (10-cup) ovenproof dish.

2 Make meat sauce; make cheese topping.

3 Cook pasta in large saucepan of boiling water until tender; drain. Combine hot pasta, egg and cheese in large bowl. Press pasta over base of dish.

4 Top pasta evenly with meat sauce; pour over cheese topping. Smooth surface; sprinkle with breadcrumbs.

5 Bake about 1 hour or until browned lightly. Stand 10 minutes before serving.

MEAT SAUCE Heat oil in large saucepan; cook onion and beef, stirring, until beef is browned. Stir in undrained tomatoes, paste, stock, wine and cinnamon; simmer, uncovered, about 20 minutes or until mixture is thick. Season. Cool; stir in egg.

CHEESE TOPPING Heat butter in medium saucepan, add flour; cook, stirring, until mixture bubbles and thickens. Remove from heat; gradually stir in milk. Stir over heat until sauce boils and thickens; stir in cheese. Season to taste. Cool 5 minutes; stir in egg yolks.

NUTRITIONAL COUNT PER SERVING 45.8g total fat (22.7g saturated fat); 3528kJ (844 cal); 52.5g carbohydrate; 52.1g protein; 4.1g fibre

BEEF BOURGUIGNON AND POTATO PIE

PREP + COOK TIME 1 HOUR 20 MINUTES   SERVES 4

500g (1 pound) minced (ground) beef
30g (1 ounce) butter
1 medium brown onion (150g), chopped finely
4 rindless bacon slices (260g), chopped finely
155g (5 ounces) button mushrooms, sliced thinly
2 cloves garlic, crushed
2 tablespoons plain (all-purpose) flour
1 cup (250ml) dry red wine
1 cup (250ml) beef stock
2 tablespoons tomato paste
2 fresh bay leaves
1kg (2 pounds) potatoes, chopped coarsely
30g (1 ounce) butter, extra
⅓ cup (80ml) pouring cream, heated

1 Heat oiled large saucepan; cook beef, stirring, until browned, then remove from pan.
2 Heat butter in same pan; cook onion, bacon, mushrooms and garlic, stirring, until vegetables soften. Return beef to pan with flour; cook, stirring, 2 minutes. Stir in wine, stock, paste and bay leaves; bring to the boil, stirring. Reduce heat; simmer, uncovered, about 45 minutes or until thickened. Discard bay leaves. Season to taste.
3 Meanwhile, boil, steam or microwave potatoes until tender; drain. Push potato through fine sieve into large bowl; stir in butter and cream until smooth. Season to taste.
4 Preheat grill (broiler).
5 Spoon beef mixture into oiled 1.5-litre (6-cup) ovenproof dish; top with potato. Grill about 5 minutes or until browned lightly.
NUTRITIONAL COUNT PER SERVING 41.7g total fat (22.1g saturated fat); 3148kJ (753 cal); 36.6g carbohydrate; 45.1g protein; 5.8g fibre

BAKED LAMB AND SAGE CREPES

PREP + COOK TIME 1 HOUR 10 MINUTES (+ STANDING)   SERVES 4

1 medium brown onion (150g), chopped finely

2 cloves garlic, chopped finely

3 rindless bacon slices (240g), chopped coarsely

500g (1 pound) minced (ground) lamb

½ cup (125ml) dry red wine

2 tablespoons tomato paste

½ cup (75g) seeded black olives

2 tablespoons finely shredded fresh sage

1¼ cups (310ml) bottled tomato pasta sauce

1 cup (100g) pizza cheese

SAGE CREPE BATTER

1½ cups (375ml) milk

30g (1 ounce) butter

2 eggs

1 cup (150g) plain (all-purpose) flour

1 tablespoon finely chopped fresh sage

1 Make sage crêpe batter.

2 Heat large oiled frying pan; cook onion, garlic and bacon, stirring, until onion softens. Add lamb; cook, stirring, until browned. Stir in wine and paste; bring to the boil. Reduce heat; simmer, uncovered, stirring occasionally, about 20 minutes or until sauce thickens. Remove from heat; stir in olives and sage. Season.

3 Pour ¼-cup crêpe batter into heated oiled frying pan (base measures 15cm/6 inches); cook until bubbles begin to appear on surface. Turn crêpe, cook until browned lightly; transfer to a plate. Repeat with remaining batter to make eight crêpes.

4 Preheat oven to 220°C/425°F.

5 Place one crêpe on board; spread ½ cup lamb mixture across centre of crêpe. Roll crêpe tightly to enclose filling; place, seam-side down, in shallow 20cm x 30cm (8-inch x 12-inch) ovenproof dish. Repeat with remaining crêpes and mince mixture. Pour pasta sauce over crêpes; sprinkle with cheese.

6 Bake crêpes, covered, 15 minutes; uncover, bake about 5 minutes or until browned lightly.

SAGE CREPE BATTER Heat milk and butter in small saucepan until butter is melted; cool. Whisk eggs into milk mixture. Sift flour into medium bowl; stir in sage. Gradually whisk milk mixture into flour mixture until batter is smooth. Cover batter; stand 1 hour. The consistency should be like thin pouring cream; if not, add a little more milk.

NUTRITIONAL COUNT PER SERVING 39.6g total fat (19.7g saturated fat); 3386kJ (810 cal); 48.6g carbohydrate; 57.4g protein; 4.6g fibre

SERVING SUGGESTION Serve with a green salad.

TIPS Leftover bolognese sauce can be used in place of the lamb mixture. We used a thin tomato pasta sauce, also known as sugo or passata, which contains only tomatoes and onion.

BABY ROCKET QUICHE

PREP + COOK TIME 1 HOUR 20 MINUTES
(+ REFRIGERATION & COOLING) SERVES 8

50g (1½ ounces) baby rocket (arugula) leaves, chopped finely
3 eggs • 1 egg yolk • ¾ cup (180ml) pouring cream
PASTRY
1¼ cups (185g) plain (all-purpose) flour
125g (4 ounces) cold butter, chopped coarsely
1 egg yolk • 2 teaspoons iced water

1 Make pastry.
2 Preheat oven to 200°C/400°F.
3 Grease shallow 20cm (8-inch) round loose-based flan tin. Roll pastry on floured surface until 5mm (¼ inch) thick. Ease pastry into tin, press into base and side. Cover; refrigerate 20 minutes.
4 Line pastry with baking paper; fill with dried beans or rice. Bake 12 minutes. Carefully remove paper and rice; bake about 8 minutes **or** until pastry is browned lightly. Reduce oven to 160°C/325°F.
5 Sprinkle rocket into pastry case. Whisk eggs, egg yolk and cream in medium jug, season; pour over rocket. Bake 40 minutes or until set. Cool.
PASTRY Process flour and butter until crumbly. With motor operating, add egg yolk and enough of the water until ingredients come together. Turn pastry onto floured surface; knead gently until smooth. Wrap pastry in plastic; refrigerate 20 minutes.
NUTRITIONAL COUNT PER SERVING 25.9g total fat (15.6g saturated fat); 1375kJ (329 cal); 17.6g carbohydrate; 6.7g protein; 1g fibre

CHICKEN SCHNITZEL

PREP + COOK TIME 35 MINUTES SERVES 4

4 chicken breast fillets (800g)
¼ cup (35g) plain (all-purpose) flour • 2 eggs
1 tablespoon milk • 2½ cups (175g) stale white breadcrumbs
2 teaspoons finely grated lemon rind
2 tablespoons each finely chopped fresh basil and
flat-leaf parsley
⅓ cup (25g) finely grated parmesan cheese
vegetable oil, for shallow-frying

1 Using meat mallet, gently pound chicken, one piece at a time, between sheets of plastic wrap until 5mm (¼-inch) thick; cut each piece in half.
2 Whisk flour, eggs and milk in shallow bowl; combine breadcrumbs, rind, herbs and cheese in another shallow bowl. Coat chicken pieces, one at a time, in egg mixture then breadcrumb mixture.
3 Heat oil in large frying pan; shallow-fry chicken, in batches, until cooked. Drain on absorbent paper.
NUTRITIONAL COUNT PER SERVING 27.4g total fat (5.8g saturated fat); 2629kJ (629 cal); 36.6g carbohydrate; 57.7g protein; 2.4g fibre
SERVING SUGGESTION Serve with green beans and lemon wedges.

Sunbeam ELECTRIC FRYPAN

Bench top appliances made a dramatic entrance to the home during the fifties providing diversification of cooking styles and, of course, making life easier for the home cook.
Advertisement featured in The Australian Women's Weekly magazine circa 1957

MAKES MEALS TO REMEMBER!

TO-MORROW IN YOUR OWN KITCHEN

Yes, in your own kitchen, *you* can cook delicious meals to the same glorious perfection shown in the natural colour photograph above. Don't delay another day — be one of the hundreds of wise women who cook the modern, wonderful, Sunbeam way. Buy *your* Electric Frypan tomorrow!

EVERY MEAL EVERY DAY FOR EVER AFTER

This is the fabulous frying pan that *not only fries,* but grills, braises, roasts, bakes, casseroles, etc. You'll use it for breakfast, lunch and dinner; you'll use it for snacks and suppers, too! In fact, you'll use it so often that you'll wonder how you ever did without one!

AUTOMATIC HEAT CONTROL IS THE SECRET

The handle contains the *super-accurate* Sunbeam thermostat which has made this appliance the rage of Australian kitchens. Scientifically correct temperatures are clearly indicated for each cooking operation. Set the dial — switch on . . . then watch the food cook perfectly, the automatic Sunbeam way.

BUY THIS *FABULOUS* APPLIANCE ON EASY TERMS AT SUNBEAM DEALERS.

8

DINNER WITH THE *Joneses*

IN POST-WAR AUSTRALIA, EATING OUT WAS NOT COMMON, BUT DINNER PARTIES WITH FRIENDS AND FAMILY WERE. THESE WERE RATHER GRAND AFFAIRS WITH THE MENU PLANNED DAYS IN ADVANCE. THESE PARTIES WERE THE PERFECT OCCASIONS FOR TRYING STYLISH NEW RECIPES FROM THE PAGES OF MAGAZINES SUCH AS *THE AUSTRALIAN WOMEN'S WEEKLY*. ENTREES WERE CONSIDERED THE HEIGHT OF FASHION, AND A LAVISH DESSERT CONCLUDED THE EVENING.

DUCK A L'ORANGE

PREP + COOK TIME 1 HOUR 55 MINUTES   SERVES 4

2kg (4-pound) whole duck

30g (1 ounce) butter, melted

1 large orange (300g)

1 tablespoon caster (superfine) sugar

1 tablespoon white vinegar

2 teaspoons lemon juice

2 cups (500ml) chicken stock

2 teaspoons arrowroot

1 tablespoon water

½ cup (125ml) orange-flavoured liqueur

1 Preheat oven to 180°C/350°F.

2 Rinse duck under cold water; pat dry inside and out with absorbent paper. Tie legs together with kitchen string; tuck wings under duck. Place duck in oiled large baking dish; brush butter all over duck, season. Roast, uncovered, about 1 hour, basting occasionally.

3 Meanwhile, peel orange thinly. Discard any white pith from peel; cut peel into thin strips. Reserve ½ cup juice from orange.

4 Combine rind, orange juice, sugar, vinegar, lemon juice and stock in medium saucepan; bring to the boil. Boil, uncovered, without stirring, until liquid is reduced by half. Gradually stir in blended arrowroot and the water; cook, stirring, until sauce almost boils and thickens. Remove from heat; stir in liqueur.

5 Remove baking dish from oven; drain pan juices from dish. Pour orange sauce over duck; roast, uncovered, a further 30 minutes, basting with sauce occasionally, until duck is tender and well-glazed.

6 Serve duck with orange sauce.

NUTRITIONAL COUNT PER SERVING 22.5g total fat (9.2g saturated fat); 2420kJ (579 cal); 23.3g carbohydrate; 57.5g protein; 0.2g fibre

SERVING SUGGESTION Serve with steamed green beans, potatoes and carrots.

CLASSIC RETRO RECIPE

STEAK DIANE

PREP + COOK TIME 20 MINUTES   SERVES 4

1 tablespoon olive oil
4 x 150g (4½-ounce) beef fillet steaks
⅓ cup (80ml) brandy
2 cloves garlic, crushed
¼ cup (60ml) worcestershire sauce
1 cup (250ml) pouring cream
1 tablespoon finely chopped
   fresh flat-leaf parsley

1 Heat oil in large frying pan; cook steaks until cooked as desired. Remove from pan; cover to keep warm.
2 Add brandy to pan; bring to the boil. Add garlic, sauce and cream; cook, stirring, 3 minutes or until sauce thickens slightly.
3 Remove pan from heat; stir in parsley, season to taste.
4 Serve steaks with sauce.

NUTRITIONAL COUNT PER SERVING 40.6g total fat (22.3g saturated fat); 2324kJ (556 cal); 5.2g carbohydrate; 33.2g protein; 0.4g fibre

SERVING SUGGESTION Serve with shoestring chips and a leafy green salad.

GOAT'S CHEESE GATEAU

PREP + COOK TIME 1 HOUR (+ REFRIGERATION & COOLING) SERVES 16

½ cup (140g) bottled roasted red capsicum (bell pepper), drained
250g (8 ounces) cream cheese, softened
2 tablespoons lemon juice
360g (11½ ounces) goat's cheese, softened
¼ cup (60ml) pouring cream
1 tablespoon finely chopped preserved lemon rind
2 teaspoons finely grated lemon rind
2 tablespoons finely chopped fresh chervil

GRAPE JUICE GLAZE
¾ cup (180ml) grape juice
2 teaspoons gelatine
1 tablespoon caster (superfine) sugar
¼ cup (60ml) port

1 Grease 20cm (8-inch) springform tin; line base and side with baking paper.
2 Blend or process capsicum, cream cheese and half the juice until combined; season to taste. Spread into tin. Cover; refrigerate 30 minutes.
3 Blend or process goat's cheese, cream, preserved lemon, lemon rind, chervil and remaining juice until combined; season to taste. Spread evenly over capsicum mixture. Cover; refrigerate 30 minutes.
4 Meanwhile, make grape juice glaze; cool.
5 Pour glaze over cheese mixture. Cover; refrigerate overnight.
6 Remove gateau from pan; serve cold with bagel crisps and salad leaves.

GRAPE JUICE GLAZE Place ¼ cup of the grape juice and the gelatine in a small heatproof jug. Stand jug in pan of simmering water; stir until gelatine is dissolved, cool. Stir remaining grape juice and sugar in small saucepan over low heat until sugar dissolves; cool, then stir in the port and the gelatine mixture.

NUTRITIONAL COUNT PER SERVING 10.4g total fat (6.7g saturated fat); 556kJ (133 cal); 4.4g carbohydrate; 4.9g protein; 0.2g fibre

TIP Preserved lemons can be bought from delis and some supermarkets. Remove a piece of lemon from the jar, discard the lemon flesh. Rinse the rind under water, dry, then chop finely.

CHICKEN TERRINE

PREP + COOK TIME 1 HOUR 20 MINUTES
(+ REFRIGERATION) SERVES 8

14 slices prosciutto (210g)
600g (1¼ pounds) chicken thigh fillets
600g (1¼ pounds) chicken breast fillets
¼ cup (35g) unsalted pistachios, chopped coarsely
3 teaspoons dijon mustard
1 teaspoon finely grated lemon rind
¼ cup coarsely chopped fresh flat-leaf parsley

1 Preheat oven to 200°C/400°F. Oil 8cm x 20cm (3¼-inch x 8-inch) loaf
pan; line base and two long sides with baking paper, extending paper
5cm (2 inches) over sides.
2 Line base and sides of pan with prosciutto, slightly overlapping the
slices and allowing overhang on long sides of pan.
3 Chop chicken into 2cm (¾-inch) pieces. Process half the chicken
until minced finely. Combine chicken mince, chopped chicken and
remaining ingredients in large bowl; season. Press into pan. Fold
prosciutto and baking paper over to cover; cover tightly with foil.
4 Place pan in medium baking dish; pour in enough boiling water to
come halfway up side of pan. Bake terrine 1 hour. Drain juices from pan.
Cool; weight with another dish filled with heavy cans. Refrigerate 3 hours.
5 Turn terrine onto plate; slice thickly to serve.
NUTRITIONAL COUNT PER SERVING 13.3g total fat
(3.7g saturated fat); 1116kJ (267 cal);
0.8g carbohydrate; 35.7g protein; 0.5g fibre

MELON IN PROSCIUTTO

PREP TIME 15 MINUTES   SERVES 4

1 small rockmelon (1.3kg), halved lengthways
12 slices prosciutto (180g)
2 tablespoons olive oil
¼ cup loosely packed fresh flat-leaf parsley leaves

1 Peel and seed rockmelon; cut into 12 wedges.
2 Wrap prosciutto around melon wedges.
3 Serve melon drizzled with oil and sprinkled with parsley.
NUTRITIONAL COUNT PER SERVING 11.9g total fat (2.2g saturated fat);
802kJ (192 cal); 10.9g carbohydrate; 9.4g protein; 2.5g fibre
TIP Use a good-quality extra virgin olive oil for the best flavour.

While Australians were not large consumers of wine during the fifties, fortified wines such as sherry and port were familiar. Gradually, well known brands began to introduce different varieties such as champagne.
Advertisement featured in The Australian Women's Weekly magazine circa 1953

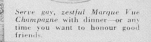

Serve gay, zestful Marque Vue Champagne with dinner—or any time you want to honour good friends.

M°WILLIAM'S *Wines*

Do the Christmas honours with these great wines!

Wine is the very heart of Christmas good cheer. It is a traditional part of the festivities and McWilliam's provide a range of great wines that do full justice to the occasion. Whichever McWilliam's wines you choose you will find full flavour and rich bouquet and the delicious qualities of Australia's choicest vintages. **Obtainable wherever wine is sold.**

CHARCUTERIE PLATE

PREP + COOK TIME **45 MINUTES** SERVES **10**

1 tablespoon finely chopped fresh tarragon

2 tablespoons olive oil

24 cherry tomatoes (250g)

1 loaf sourdough bread (675g), sliced thickly

150g (4½ ounces) each thinly sliced prosciutto, salami and pastrami

120g (4 ounces) chicken liver pâté

PICKLED MUSHROOMS

2 tablespoons olive oil

50g (1½ ounces) fresh shiitake mushrooms, trimmed

70g (2½ ounces) swiss brown mushrooms, quartered

100g (3 ounces) enoki mushrooms, trimmed

3 fresh small red thai (serrano) chillies

4 sprigs fresh thyme

1 tablespoon caster (superfine) sugar

2 tablespoons sherry vinegar

CARROT AND TURMERIC SALAD

1 large carrot (180g), cut into matchsticks

¾ cup (225g) mayonnaise

2 teaspoons finely grated lime rind

2 teaspoons lime juice

1 teaspoon ground turmeric

1 teaspoon yellow mustard seeds, toasted

2 tablespoons finely chopped fresh chives

1 Make pickled mushrooms.

2 Make carrot and turmeric salad.

3 Combine tarragon and oil in medium bowl; season to taste. Add tomatoes; mix gently.

4 Char-grill or toast sourdough.

5 Serve tomato mixture, sliced meats, pâté and toasts with mushrooms and salad.

PICKLED MUSHROOMS Heat oil in large frying pan; cook mushrooms, chillies and thyme, stirring, over medium heat, 1 minute. Stir in sugar then vinegar; cook, stirring, until mushrooms are tender. Cool, season to taste.

CARROT AND TURMERIC SALAD Combine ingredients in medium bowl; season to taste.

NUTRITIONAL COUNT PER SERVING 27.4g total fat (5.7g saturated fat); 2103kJ (503 cal); 43.2g carbohydrate; 18.7g protein; 5g fibre

TIPS A charcuterie plate consists of cured or prepared meats (most often pork). To save time, purchase various preserves and dips from the supermarket instead of making the pickled mushrooms and carrot salad. Water crackers and oat cakes can be served instead of the sourdough.

1) Tinned ... imps ... in place ...
a thick ... of ...

2) Salami ... with scrambled ...
and cuc ... or twist ... egg ...
been scr ... ed rather firmly ...
Danish s ... ad then cut into ...
strips)

3) Ham with scr ... ... and to
mato twists

4) Danish Blue cheese ...

8) Luncheon meat ... in hard-
folded tri ...

ON THE DISH

1) Cold chicken garnished with tomato and cucumber twists

2) Cold boiled bacon or ham with Russian salad
(Recipe No. 438)

3) Danish Blue cheese

4) Tongue with curried Russian salad (add a little
curry powder to the mayonnaise in the Russian salad)

1034 DANISH SANDWICH PARTY

1035 ASSORTED CHEESE TRAY

Prepare a soft cheese spread, by
mixing grated cheese (Dutch Gouda
is good for this) with mayonnaise.
Season well and use for:

Ham and Asparagus Rolls Spread
slices of ham with the mixture and
roll round asparagus tips

Savoury Dates Fill stoned dates, and
top with paprika pepper

Ribbon Sandwiches Spread thin slices
of rye or wholemeal bread. Make
a three-decker sandwich and cut
into tiny shapes

Coconut balls Roll mixture into small
balls and coat with desiccated coconut

Savoury Biscuits Spread on crisp biscuits, top with salted nuts or tomato

Original recipes and photographs from the iconic *The Australian Women's Weekly Cookery In Colour*, published in 1960 by *The Australian Women's Weekly* in conjunction with Paul Hamlyn, London.

TAIL PARTY SAVOURIES

...ll and easy to eat, since it is very difficult ...ss and try to hold food at the same time. ...fillings, etc. must be firm. Cheese and ...ases can be made beforehand and kept in

Savoury Boats

...pastry (Recipe No. 1026). Roll out, fill and ...at shapes with the pastry. Pipe with ham ...pe No. 1038), decorate with strips of tomato ...er and coat with aspic jelly.

Ham Butter

...ham or bacon   2 oz. butter or substitute

...nce and sieve the ham. Work in butter and mix ...ch paste.

Ham Savouries

...rounds of cheese pastry (Recipe No. 1026). Bake ...ted until crisp or golden-brown. Lay a round of ...cooked bacon, pipe with sieved cream cheese and ...e with tomato coated with aspic.

Ham Butterflies

...ut rounds of cheese pastry (Recipe No. 1026), and ...half of these to make wings. Pipe with ham butter ...pe No. 1038). Decorate wings of cheese pastry with ...er and coat with aspic jelly.

Radish Crowns

...t out rounds of cheese pastry (Recipe No. 1026). Bake ...directed. Pipe with ham butter (Recipe No. 1038), ...corate with slices of radish and coat with aspic jelly.

Bacon Bouchées and Fingers

...042

...ill cooked bouchées (tiny vol-au-vent cases) of cheese ...pastry (Recipe No. 1026) or puff pastry (Recipe No. 588) ...with chopped lean bacon mixed with aspic, pipe with ...sieved cream cheese, decorate with fancy shapes cut out ...of cucumber skin and coat with aspic jelly.

Kebabs

1043

Arrange on cocktail sticks cooked bacon rolls or cubes of ham, pineapple chunks, cubes of cheese, slices of cooked sausage, gherkins and button onions. Serve cold, or brush with melted butter and grill gently for 5 minutes.

Bacon Titbits

1044

Remove rind from streaky rashers, cut each in half, and spread with mustard or chutney. Roll round any of these: a cube of cheese or pineapple; a cocktail sausage or a prawn; sweet gherkins or stuffed olives; a piece of banana or a date. Place on a cocktail stick, grill or bake until the bacon is cooked. Serve hot or cold.

Ham Bites

1045

Spread thin slices of ham or lean bacon with cream cheese or peanut butter, seasoned with grated onion ... horse-radish sauce. Roll up tightly, leave in ref... or a cold place for several hours. Cut into bi...

RARE ROAST BEEF WITH ANCHOVY BUTTER

PREP + COOK TIME **1 HOUR 25 MINUTES (+ REFRIGERATION)** SERVES 8

½ cup (125ml) barbecue sauce

2 cloves garlic, crushed

1 tablespoon finely chopped fresh rosemary

⅓ cup (80ml) olive oil

2kg (4-pound) boneless beef sirloin

300g (9½ ounces) yellow beans, trimmed

300g (9½ ounces) green beans, trimmed

800g (1½ pounds) button mushrooms

2 tablespoons finely chopped fresh chives

ANCHOVY BUTTER

200g (6½ ounces) butter, softened

4 shallots (100g), chopped finely

1 tablespoon dijon mustard

1 tablespoon finely chopped fresh tarragon

5 drained anchovy fillets, chopped finely

1 teaspoon sumac

1 Preheat oven to 220°C/425°F.

2 Make anchovy butter.

3 Combine sauce, garlic, rosemary and 2 tablespoons of the oil in small bowl; rub all over beef. Place beef on oiled wire rack over baking dish; pour in enough water to half fill the dish.

4 Roast beef about 45 minutes or until cooked to your liking. Cover beef loosely with foil; stand 10 minutes before slicing thickly.

5 Boil, steam or microwave beans until tender; drain.

6 Heat remaining oil in large frying pan; cook mushrooms, stirring, over medium heat, until tender.

7 Combine mushrooms, beans and chives in large bowl; season.

8 Divide bean mixture among serving plates; top with beef and slices of anchovy butter.

ANCHOVY BUTTER Beat butter in medium bowl with electric mixer until soft; beat in remaining ingredients, season to taste. Form into log, roll in plastic wrap; refrigerate until firm.

NUTRITIONAL COUNT PER SERVING 45.8g total fat (21.6g saturated fat); 2897kJ (693 cal); 11.8g carbohydrate; 57.5g protein; 5g fibre

Imperial LUNCHEON BEEF

VEAL CUTLETS WITH SAGE AND GARLIC BUTTER

CHILLI PRAWN LINGUINE

PREP + COOK TIME 20 MINUTES (+ REFRIGERATION) SERVES 4

1 medium lemon (140g) • 2 cloves garlic, crushed
1 tablespoon fresh sage leaves
¼ cup (60ml) olive oil • 8 veal cutlets (1kg)
GARLIC BUTTER
125g (4 ounces) butter, softened • 2 cloves garlic, crushed
4 drained anchovy fillets, chopped finely
1 teaspoon finely chopped fresh sage

1 Peel rind thinly from lemon; cut rind into long, thin strips.
Combine lemon with garlic, sage, oil and veal in large bowl.
Cover; refrigerate 3 hours or overnight.
2 Make garlic butter.
3 Cook veal on heated oiled grill plate (or grill or barbecue).
Serve with garlic butter.
GARLIC BUTTER Combine ingredients in small bowl; season to taste.
NUTRITIONAL COUNT PER SERVING 45.6g total fat (26.6g saturated fat);
2554kJ (611 cal); 0.8g carbohydrate; 50g protein; 0.9g fibre
SERVING SUGGESTION Serve with a mixed leaf salad.

PREP + COOK TIME 25 MINUTES SERVES 6

1.5kg (3 pounds) uncooked small king prawns (shrimp)
500g (1 pound) linguine pasta • ¼ cup (60ml) olive oil
3 cloves garlic, sliced thinly
2 fresh long red chillies, sliced thinly
⅓ cup coarsely chopped fresh flat-leaf parsley
50g (1½ ounces) baby rocket (arugula) leaves

1 Shell and devein prawns, leaving tails intact.
2 Cook pasta in large saucepan of boiling water until just tender.
3 Meanwhile, heat half the oil in large frying pan; cook prawns, in
batches, until changed in colour. Remove from pan; cover to keep warm.
4 Heat remaining oil in same pan; cook garlic and chilli, stirring,
about 1 minute or until fragrant.
5 Reserve ½ cup of the pasta cooking liquid then drain pasta.
Return pasta to pan with prawns, reserved cooking liquid, chilli
mixture, parsley and rocket; season to taste, toss to combine.
NUTRITIONAL COUNT PER SERVING 10.9g total fat (1.6g saturated fat);
2002kJ (479 cal); 57.2g carbohydrate; 35.3g protein; 3.3g fibre

KUMARA GNOCCHI
WITH ROCKET AND BASIL PESTO

PREP + COOK TIME 1 HOUR 10 MINUTES (+ REFRIGERATION) SERVES 4

2 medium unpeeled kumara (orange sweet potato) (800g)

4 small unpeeled desiree potatoes (480g)

1 cup (150g) plain (all-purpose) flour

1 egg yolk

ROCKET AND BASIL PESTO

2 tablespoons olive oil

2 tablespoons finely grated parmesan cheese

1 clove garlic, quartered

2 tablespoons lemon juice

50g (1½ounces) baby rocket (arugula) leaves

1 cup firmly packed fresh basil leaves

1 Boil, steam or microwave kumara and potatoes, separately, until tender; drain. Peel when cool enough to handle; chop coarsely. Using wooden spoon, push kumara and potato through fine sieve into large bowl.

2 Stir flour and yolk into kumara mixture then knead dough gently on floured surface until mixture comes together. Divide dough into four portions. Roll each portion into 40cm (16-inch) log; cut each log into 24 pieces. Roll each piece into a ball; roll balls, one at a time, along the inside tines of a floured fork, pressing gently on top of dough with index finger to form gnocchi shape (grooved on one side and dimpled on the other). Place gnocchi, in single layer, on floured trays. Cover; refrigerate 1 hour.

3 Meanwhile, make rocket and basil pesto.

4 Cook gnocchi, in batches, uncovered, in large saucepan of boiling water about 3 minutes or until gnocchi float to the surface. Remove gnocchi with slotted spoon. Gently toss gnocchi in large bowl with pesto.

ROCKET AND BASIL PESTO Blend or process ingredients until smooth; season to taste.

NUTRITIONAL COUNT PER SERVING 12.6g total fat (2.5g saturated fat); 1914kJ (458 cal); 71.8g carbohydrate; 13.4g protein; 8g fibre

SERVING SUGGESTION Serve topped with baby rocket leaves.

TIP This gnocchi dough is very soft, so you'll need an extra ½ cup of plain (all-purpose) flour for the board when kneading and rolling to prevent it from sticking.

OVEN-BAKED FISH WITH LEMON AND MINT RISOTTO

PREP + COOK TIME **40 MINUTES** SERVES 6

1 litre (4 cups) vegetable stock
½ cup (125ml) water
20g (¾ ounce) butter
2 tablespoons olive oil
1 large brown onion (200g), chopped finely
1½ cups (300g) arborio rice
⅓ cup (80ml) dry white wine
6 x 180g (5½-ounce) white fish fillets, skin on
⅓ cup finely chopped fresh mint leaves
1 tablespoon fresh lemon thyme leaves
2 teaspoons finely grated lemon rind
2 tablespoons lemon juice
30g (1 ounce) butter, extra
⅓ cup (25g) finely grated parmesan cheese

1 Place stock and the water in medium saucepan; bring to the boil. Reduce heat; simmer, covered.
2 Heat butter and half the oil in large saucepan; cook onion, stirring, until soft. Add rice; stir to coat rice in onion mixture. Add wine; bring to the boil. Reduce heat; simmer, stirring, until liquid is almost evaporated.
3 Stir 1 cup of the simmering stock mixture into rice mixture; cook, stirring, over low heat, until liquid is absorbed. Continue adding stock mixture in 1-cup batches, stirring until absorbed after each addition. Total cooking time will be about 35 minutes or until rice is tender.
4 Meanwhile, preheat oven to 180°C/350°F. Line oven tray with baking paper.
5 About 10 minutes before risotto is cooked, heat remaining oil in large frying pan. Cook fish, skin-side down, until skin is browned and crisp; turn, cook 1 minute. Transfer fillets to oven tray, skin-side up; cook in oven about 7 minutes.
6 Stir herbs, rind, juice, extra butter and cheese into risotto; season to taste.
7 Divide risotto among serving dishes; top with fish. Serve topped with a little more butter, some finely sliced lemon rind and a few lemon thyme leaves.

NUTRITIONAL COUNT PER SERVING 20.3g total fat (8.6g saturated fat); 1910kJ (457 cal); 42.9g carbohydrate; 44.9g protein; 1.1g fibre
TIPS We used barramundi, but you can use any white fish fillets. The most time-consuming part of making this risotto is the stirring. Have the ingredients ready to add and involve your guests, even if it's sharing a chat and a glass of wine as you stir.

CAJUN CHICKENS WITH SPICY TOMATO SALSA

PREP + COOK TIME 1 HOUR 40 MINUTES   SERVES 6

6 x 500g (1-pound) small chickens (poussin)
2 tablespoons olive oil
1 small white onion (80g), grated coarsely
2 cloves garlic, crushed
2 tablespoons sweet paprika
2 teaspoons each ground cinnamon and ground fennel
2 teaspoons dried oregano
SPICY TOMATO SALSA
6 large egg (plum) tomatoes (540g), halved
1 tablespoon olive oil
1 medium brown onion (150g), chopped finely
2 cloves garlic, crushed
1 tablespoon sweet paprika
1 teaspoon smoked paprika
1 tablespoon red wine vinegar
1 fresh long red chilli, chopped finely

1 Discard necks from chickens. Using scissors, cut along each side of each chicken's backbone; discard backbones. Turn chickens skin-side up; press down on breastbone to flatten.
2 Combine remaining ingredients in small bowl; season. Rub mixture all over chickens.
3 Cook chickens on heated oiled grill plate (or grill or barbecue), turning halfway through cooking time, about 1 hour or until cooked.
4 Meanwhile, make spicy tomato salsa.
5 Serve chickens with salsa.
SPICY TOMATO SALSA Cook tomato on heated oiled grill plate, turning, until softened; chop tomato coarsely. Heat oil in medium saucepan; cook onion and garlic, stirring, until onion softens. Add spices; cook, stirring, until fragrant. Stir in tomato, vinegar and chilli; cook, uncovered, stirring occasionally, about 20 minutes or until salsa thickens. Season to taste.
NUTRITIONAL COUNT PER SERVING 49.5g total fat (13.8g saturated fat); 2788kJ (667 cal); 4g carbohydrate; 51.4g protein; 1.9g fibre
TIPS You can prepare and marinate the chickens the day before. Store, covered, in refrigerator. Bring the chickens out of the fridge 20 minutes before cooking.
You can also make the salsa the day before. Store refrigerated in an airtight container. Reheat over medium heat when ready to serve. This recipe also works with three whole chickens but the cooking time will be longer.
Don't waste the chicken necks and backbones – use them to make stock.

LUNCH ON SUNDAY

SUNDAYS WERE FAMILY DAYS AND NO WEEK WAS COMPLETE WITHOUT SUNDAY LUNCH, A TIME FOR THE EXTENDED FAMILY TO GATHER AROUND THE DINING TABLE TO ENJOY A MEAL AND DISCUSS THE EVENTS OF THE WEEK GONE BY. THE CENTREPIECE WAS THE SUNDAY ROAST, COMPLETE WITH ALL THE TRIMMINGS. LAMB AND BEEF WERE POPULAR, WITH POULTRY BEING RESERVED FOR SPECIAL OCCASIONS. FRUIT AND ICE-CREAM WAS A FAVOURITE TO END THE MEAL.

GUARD OF HONOUR

PREP + COOK TIME 1 HOUR   SERVES 4

½ cup each firmly packed fresh flat-leaf parsley
   and mint leaves
¼ cup loosely packed fresh oregano leaves
4 cloves garlic, chopped coarsely
⅓ cup (80ml) olive oil
2 x 8 french-trimmed lamb cutlet racks (720g)
1kg (2 pounds) baby new potatoes

1 Preheat oven to 200°C/400°F.

2 Blend or process herbs, garlic and half the oil until smooth; season to taste. Place lamb racks in large oiled baking dish, leaning against one another, interlacing cutlet bones, so racks stand upright. Press herb mixture onto each rack.

3 Meanwhile, boil, steam or microwave potatoes until just tender; drain. Cut potatoes in half, place on oiled oven tray; drizzle with remaining oil, season.

4 Roast lamb and potatoes, uncovered, about 35 minutes or until lamb is cooked as desired. Remove lamb from oven, cover; stand 10 minutes. Roast potatoes a further 10 minutes or until browned lightly.

5 Serve lamb with potatoes.

NUTRITIONAL COUNT PER SERVING 26.9g total fat (6.6g saturated fat); 2086kJ (499 cal); 33.6g carbohydrate; 26.7g protein; 6.3g fibre

SERVING SUGGESTION Serve with steamed vegetables.

TIPS You can use skewers or toothpicks to help keep the guard of honour secure.

Wrap the ends of cutlet bones with small pieces of foil to stop them burning during roasting. If you want to decorate the racks with 'paper booties', put them on after removing lamb racks from the oven.

CLASSIC RETRO RECIPE

BEEF WELLINGTON

PREP + COOK TIME 1 HOUR 20 MINUTES (+ COOLING) SERVES 4

800g (1½-pound) piece beef fillet
1 tablespoon olive oil
25g (¾ ounce) butter
1 small brown onion (80g), chopped finely
125g (4 ounces) button mushrooms, chopped finely
150g (4½ ounces) chicken or duck liver pâté
2 sheets puff pastry
1 egg, beaten lightly

1 Tie beef securely with kitchen string. Heat oil in large frying pan; cook beef until browned all over. Wrap beef in foil; cool.

2 Heat butter in same pan; cook onion and mushrooms, stirring, until tender. Cool.

3 Preheat oven to 240°C/425°F. Line oven tray with baking paper.

4 Stir pâté in medium bowl until soft. Remove string from beef. Spread pâté all over beef; season.

5 Roll out pastry on lightly floured surface into a rectangle large enough to enclose beef; moisten edges with water. Place mushroom mixture down centre of pastry; place beef on top of mushrooms. Fold pastry over beef to enclose; trim excess pastry and press edges to seal. Place beef, seam-side down, on tray; brush with egg then cut small slits in top of pastry.

6 Bake beef 10 minutes. Reduce oven to 200°C/400°F; bake a further 20 minutes or until browned lightly. Serve beef, sliced thickly.

NUTRITIONAL COUNT PER SERVING 52.2g total fat (23g saturated fat); 3449kJ (825 cal); 31.9g carbohydrate; 56.4g protein; 2.7g fibre

SERVING SUGGESTION Serve with steamed vegetables.

TIPS It is important to trim excess pastry when covering the beef. Don't have the pastry too thick at the joins or the pastry will not cook through. To decorate, cut small leaves from pastry scraps and secure them to the beef wellington with a little of the egg before baking.

ROAST CHICKEN WITH TARRAGON CREAM

PREP + COOK TIME 50 MINUTES   SERVES 8

8 chicken drumettes (560g)
8 chicken wingettes (440g)
1 medium red onion (170g), chopped finely
1 clove garlic, crushed
1 dried bay leaf
½ cup (125ml) dry white wine
½ cup (125ml) water

TARRAGON CREAM
¼ cup (60g) packaged cream cheese, softened
1 tablespoon coarsely chopped fresh tarragon
1 tablespoon lemon juice
¼ cup (75g) mayonnaise
2 tablespoons warm water

1 Preheat oven to 200°C/400°F.
2 Cook chicken, in batches, in heated oiled large flameproof baking dish until browned all over. Remove from dish.
3 Cook onion and garlic in same dish, stirring, until onion softens. Return chicken to dish with bay leaf, wine and the water; bring to the boil.
4 Transfer dish to oven; roast, uncovered, about 35 minutes or until chicken is cooked through.
5 Meanwhile, make tarragon cream.
6 Serve chicken with tarragon cream.

TARRAGON CREAM Beat cream cheese until smooth; stir in remaining ingredients. Season to taste.

NUTRITIONAL COUNT PER SERVING 11.7g total fat (3.9g saturated fat); 1003kJ (240 cal); 3.4g carbohydrate; 27.6g protein; 0.4g fibre

VEAL RACK WITH ROASTED MUSHROOM SAUCE

PREP + COOK TIME 1 HOUR 25 MINUTES   SERVES 4

1kg (2-pound) veal rack
¼ cup (60ml) olive oil
1kg (2 pounds) baby new potatoes
300g (9½ ounces) button mushrooms
150g (4½ ounces) shimeji or
   oyster mushrooms
2 cloves garlic, sliced thinly
2 tablespoons finely grated
   parmesan cheese
2 tablespoons plain (all-purpose) flour
1½ cups (375ml) chicken stock
⅓ cup (80ml) pouring cream
2 tablespoons coarsely chopped
   fresh flat-leaf parsley

1 Preheat oven to 200°C/400°F.

2 Place veal on oiled wire rack in shallow flameproof baking dish. Brush veal with 1 tablespoon of the oil, season. Roast veal, uncovered, basting occasionally, about 40 minutes or until cooked as desired.

3 Place potatoes in small baking dish; roast for last 30 minutes of veal cooking time.

4 Remove veal from dish; cover to keep warm. Add mushrooms, garlic and remaining oil to dish; stir to combine. Roast mushroom mixture and potatoes about 20 minutes or until potatoes are tender.

5 Sprinkle potatoes with cheese; roast a further 5 minutes or until cheese is melted.

6 Meanwhile, add flour to mushroom mixture in dish; cook, stirring, about 2 minutes or until mixture thickens and bubbles. Gradually stir in stock; cook, stirring, until sauce boils and thickens. Add cream and parsley, stir until heated through. Season to taste.

7 Serve veal with mushroom sauce and potatoes.

NUTRITIONAL COUNT PER SERVING 28.7g total fat (10.4g saturated fat); 2876kJ (688 cal); 40.1g carbohydrate; 62.3g protein; 8.4g fibre

MOROCCAN CHICKEN WITH COUSCOUS STUFFING

PREP + COOK TIME 2 HOURS 30 MINUTES (+ STANDING)   **SERVES** 4

1.6kg (3¼-pound) whole chicken
20g (¾ ounce) butter, melted
20 vine-ripened truss cherry
   tomatoes (400g)
1 tablespoon olive oil
COUSCOUS STUFFING
1 teaspoon olive oil
1 medium brown onion (150g),
   chopped finely
1½ cups (375ml) chicken stock
¼ cup (60ml) olive oil, extra
1 tablespoon finely grated
   lemon rind
¼ cup (60ml) lemon juice
1 cup (200g) couscous
½ cup (70g) roasted slivered
   almonds
1 cup (140g) seeded dried dates,
   chopped finely
1 teaspoon each smoked paprika
   and ground cinnamon
1 egg, beaten lightly

1 Make couscous stuffing.
2 Preheat oven to 200°C/400°F.
3 Rinse chicken under cold water; pat dry inside and out with absorbent paper. Fill large cavity loosely with stuffing; tie legs together with kitchen string. Place chicken on oiled wire rack over large baking dish; half fill with water. Brush chicken all over with butter, season.
4 Roast chicken, uncovered, 15 minutes. Reduce oven to 180°C/350°F; roast, uncovered, a further 1½ hours or until cooked through. Remove chicken from dish; cover, stand 20 minutes.
5 Meanwhile, place tomatoes on oven tray; drizzle with oil. Roast, uncovered, 20 minutes or until softened and browned.
6 Serve chicken with tomatoes.
COUSCOUS STUFFING Heat oil in small frying pan; cook onion, stirring, until soft. Bring stock, extra oil, rind and juice to the boil in medium saucepan. Remove from heat. Add couscous, cover; stand 5 minutes or until liquid is absorbed, fluffing with fork occasionally. Stir in onion, nuts, dates, spices and egg; season.
NUTRITIONAL COUNT PER SERVING 67.5g total fat (16.7g saturated fat); 4631kJ (1108 cal); 67.8g carbohydrate; 54.9g protein; 7.2g fibre

CUMIN ROASTED QUAIL

PREP + COOK TIME 55 MINUTES (+ REFRIGERATION) SERVES 8

6 x 160g (5-ounce) quail   1 tablespoon ground cumin
1 teaspoon dried chilli flakes   2 cloves garlic, crushed
2 tablespoons olive oil   1 tablespoon lemon juice
½ cup loosely packed fresh coriander (cilantro) leaves

1 Rinse quails under cold water; pat dry, inside and out, with absorbent paper. Using kitchen scissors, cut along each side of quails' backbones; discard backbones, cut quails in half.
2 Combine quail, cumin, chilli, garlic, oil and juice in large bowl. Cover; refrigerate 3 hours or overnight.
3 Preheat oven to 220°C/425°F.
4 Place quail, skin-side up, in single layer, in large baking dish, season; bake about 20 minutes or until cooked through.
5 Serve quail sprinkled with coriander.
NUTRITIONAL COUNT PER SERVING 11.2g total fat (2.4g saturated fat); 606kJ (145 cal); 0.1g carbohydrate; 11.2g protein; 0.1g fibre
TIPS Quail can be bought already boned, but with the bones remaining in the legs and wings. Ask the butcher or poultry shop to remove any remaining bones for you, if you like. We've chosen to leave all the bones intact for this recipe.

PORK LOIN WITH APPLE SAUCE

PREP + COOK TIME 2 HOURS (+ STANDING) SERVES 8

2.5kg (5-pound) boneless loin of pork, rind on
2 sprigs fresh rosemary   1 tablespoon olive oil
1 tablespoon coarse cooking salt
3 large apples (600g), peeled, cored, sliced thickly
¼ cup (60ml) water   1 teaspoon white (granulated) sugar
pinch ground cinnamon

1 Preheat oven to 240°C/475°F.
2 Tie pork at 2cm (¾-inch) intervals with kitchen string; tuck rosemary under string. Place pork in large baking dish; rub with oil then salt.
3 Roast pork, uncovered, about 40 minutes or until skin blisters. Drain excess fat from dish.
4 Reduce oven to 180°C/350°F; roast pork a further 1 hour. Cover pork loosely with foil; stand 15 minutes.
5 Meanwhile, place apple and the water in medium saucepan; simmer, covered, 5 minutes. Uncover; simmer about 5 minutes or until apple is soft. Remove from heat; stir in sugar and cinnamon.
6 Serve pork with apple sauce, and roasted vegetables, if you like.
NUTRITIONAL COUNT PER SERVING 72g total fat (24.1g saturated fat); 3762kJ (900 cal); 7.7g carbohydrate; 56.7g protein; 1.1g fibre

Illustration featured in *The Australian Women's Weekly* magazine, circa 1953

Original recipes and photographs from the iconic *The Australian Women's Weekly Cookery In Colour*, published in 1960 by *The Australian Women's Weekly* in conjunction with Paul Hamlyn, London.

BACON

CORNER GAMMON
PRIME STREAKY
FLANK
BACK AND RIBS
GAMMON HOCK
TOP STREAKY
LONG BACK
SHORT BACK
TOP BACK

1. BUTT
2. SMALL HOCK FOREHOCK
3. FORE SLIPPER
4. TOP STREAKY
5. PRIME STREAKY
6. THIN STREAKY
7. FLANK
8. GAMMON SLIPPER
9. GAMMON HOCK
10. MIDDLE GAMMON
11. CORNER GAMMON
12. LONG BACK
13. OYSTER
14. SHORT BACK
15. BACK AND RIBS
16. TOP BACK
17. PRIME COLLAR
18. END COLLAR

HAM bulk pieces

Purpose	Cut to Choose	Cooking Time	Accom...
Roasting or Baking	Gammon slipper, Middle gammon, Back and ribs, Joint top streaky	25 minutes per lb. and 25 minutes over. If well done, cook like pork for 25 minutes per lb.	Mustard, Salads, Unusual garnishes such as baked apples, oranges, pineapple, etc.
Grilling or Frying	Streaky, Gammon rashers, Back and Middle rashers, Cushion	Few minutes only for thin rashers, but with thick slices of gammon cook outside fairly quickly, then reduce heat to cook through to the middle. Keep gammon well brushed with fat when grilling	Eggs, tomatoes, mushrooms, etc., for breakfast. Vegetables or salads for main meals
Boiling or Braising	Knuckle, Streaky, Gammon slipper, Gammon hock, Middle, Back, Blade, Cushion	Soak well if you want very mild flavour, then simmer gently for 20—25 minutes per lb. and 20 to 25 minutes over. Do not boil too quickly. A pressure cooker can be used (see Recipe No. 896) Ham or bacon stock is excellent for soups	Any vegetables — beans and peas are particularly good with boiled bacon Salads etc.

TO BONE MEAT

164

Carving is much easier if the meat is boned — your butcher will doubtless do this for you, but if he has not done so, it is not difficult. Use a proper boning knife with a slim but firm blade, and feel round the bone with the tip before cutting the meat — work slowly so as to avoid waste.

TO CARVE MEAT

165

GOOD CARVING TAKES PRACTICE but there are certain rules to help you.

1) Do buy a good knife — and if you have a large family or entertain a great deal, it is wise to have two knives, since the heat of the meat when cooked is inclined to blunt the knife.

2) To carve beef — cut long slices across the joint, see picture. When carving sirloin on the bone you must, however, first, remove the top bone or chine, cut the first slices along the bone, then turn joint and cut thick slices at right angles from the bone downwards,

3) To carve lamb or mutton—cut rather thicker slices, but you should see picture. The shoulder is not easy to carve, which means carving round it — follow the formation of the joint and cutting diagonal slices. starting in the centre of the joint and cutting diag... the butcher to chine, i. e. cut through bones, on loin. A... the butcher

4) To carve pork — cut downwards as for mutton. A... for mutton

5) To carve veal — most joints as beef, but shoulder as for pork. loin as for pork.

6) To carve joints of bacon ... on the bone should be carved diagonally cut across. A wh... on the bone should be carved diagon... cut across... hole ham on the bone should be downwards. the fir... cuts when the ham is large should be downwards.

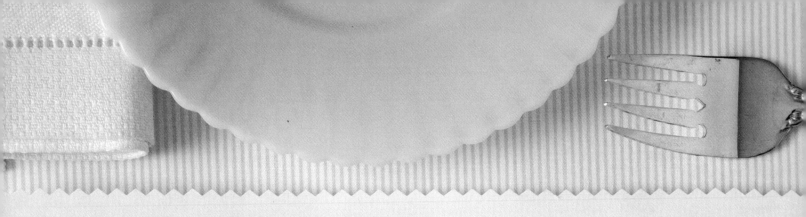

GREEK ROAST LAMB WITH SKORDALIA AND POTATOES

PREP + COOK TIME 4 HOURS 50 MINUTES (+ REFRIGERATION)   SERVES 4

2kg (4-pound) leg of lamb

2 cloves garlic, crushed

½ cup (125ml) lemon juice

2 tablespoons olive oil

1 tablespoon fresh oregano leaves

1 teaspoon fresh lemon thyme leaves

5 large potatoes (1.5kg), cut into
  2.5cm (1-inch) cubes

1 tablespoon finely grated lemon rind

2 tablespoons lemon juice, extra

2 tablespoons olive oil, extra

1 teaspoon fresh lemon thyme leaves, extra

SKORDALIA

1 medium potato (200g), quartered

3 cloves garlic, crushed

1 tablespoon lemon juice

1 tablespoon white wine vinegar

2 tablespoons water

⅓ cup (80ml) olive oil

1 Combine lamb with garlic, juice, oil, oregano and thyme in large bowl. Cover; refrigerate 3 hours or overnight.

2 Preheat oven to 160°C/325°F.

3 Place lamb in large baking dish, season; roast, uncovered, 4 hours.

4 Meanwhile, make skordalia.

5 Combine potato in large bowl with rind and extra juice, oil and thyme; season. Place potato, in single layer, on oven tray; roast for last 30 minutes of lamb cooking time.

6 Remove lamb from oven; cover to keep warm.

7 Increase oven to 220°C/425°F; roast potato a further 20 minutes or until browned lightly and cooked through.

8 Serve lamb with skordalia and potato; sprinkle with extra lemon thyme leaves.

SKORDALIA Boil, steam or microwave potato until tender; drain. Push potato through food mill or fine sieve into medium bowl; cool 10 minutes. Whisk combined garlic, juice, vinegar and the water into potato. Gradually whisk in oil in a thin, steady stream; continue whisking until skordalia thickens. Season to taste. Stir in about a tablespoon of warm water if skordalia is too thick.

NUTRITIONAL COUNT PER SERVING 57g total fat (14g saturated fat); 4556kJ (1090 cal); 51.5g carbohydrate; 91.2g protein; 6.7g fibre

STANDING RIB ROAST WITH ROAST VEGETABLES

PREP + COOK TIME 1 HOUR 50 MINUTES   SERVES 4

1.2kg (2½-pound) beef standing rib roast

¼ cup (60ml) olive oil

2 teaspoons cracked black pepper

500g (1 pound) potatoes, chopped coarsely

500g (1 pound) pumpkin, chopped coarsely

500g (1 pound) kumara (orange sweet potato), chopped coarsely

½ cup (125ml) brandy

1½ cups (375ml) beef stock

1 tablespoon cornflour (cornstarch)

¼ cup (60ml) water

1 tablespoon finely chopped fresh chives

1 Preheat oven to 200°C/400°F.

2 Tie beef, between ribs, with kitchen string. Brush beef with 1 tablespoon of the oil; sprinkle with pepper. Heat 1 tablespoon of the oil in large shallow flameproof baking dish; cook beef, uncovered, over high heat until browned all over. Transfer to oven; roast, uncovered, about 45 minutes or until cooked as desired.

3 Meanwhile, heat remaining oil in another large flameproof baking dish; cook potatoes, stirring, over high heat until browned lightly. Add pumpkin and kumara, place dish in oven with beef; roast, uncovered, about 35 minutes or until vegetables are browned. Turn off oven.

4 Place beef on vegetables, cover; return to oven to keep warm. Drain juices from beef baking dish into medium saucepan, add brandy; bring to the boil. Add stock and blended cornflour and water; cook, stirring, until sauce boils and thickens slightly. Stir in chives, season to taste; pour into medium heatproof jug.

5 Serve beef and vegetables with sauce.

NUTRITIONAL COUNT PER SERVING 29.2g total fat (8.5g saturated fat); 3114kJ (745 cal); 41.1g carbohydrate; 60.4g protein; 5.4g fibre

TIPS The best way to judge the degree of doneness for a standing rib roast is with a meat thermometer. The internal temperature should be: 55-60°C/130-140°F for rare; 60-65°C/140-150°F for medium-rare; 65-70°C/150-160°F for medium; 70-75°C/160-170°F for medium-well; and 75°C/170°F for well-done. If you don't have a meat thermometer, you can use tongs to test the roast's doneness. Gently prod or squeeze the roast – rare is very soft; medium-rare is soft; medium is springy but soft; medium-well is firm; and well-done is very firm.

GREMOLATA LAMB RACKS WITH PARSLEY AND CHILLI RISOTTO

PREP + COOK TIME **1 HOUR 10 MINUTES** SERVES 4

½ cup coarsely chopped fresh flat-leaf parsley

1 tablespoon finely grated lemon rind

⅓ cup (25g) finely grated parmesan cheese

3 cloves garlic, crushed

1 tablespoon olive oil

2 x 8 french-trimmed lamb cutlet racks (720g)

PARSLEY AND CHILLI RISOTTO

3 cups (750ml) chicken stock

3 cups (750ml) water

1 tablespoon olive oil

1 medium brown onion (150g), chopped coarsely

1½ cups (300g) arborio rice

½ cup (125ml) dry white wine

1 teaspoon finely grated lemon rind

1 fresh small red thai (serrano) chilli, chopped finely

½ cup (40g) finely grated parmesan cheese

2 cups loosely packed fresh flat-leaf parsley leaves

1 Preheat oven to 200°C/400°F.

2 Combine parsley, rind, cheese, garlic and oil in small bowl. Place lamb in oiled large shallow baking dish; press gremolata mixture onto each rack, season. Roast, uncovered, about 30 minutes or until lamb is cooked as desired.

3 Meanwhile, make parsley and chilli risotto.

4 Cut each lamb rack in half; serve with risotto.

PARSLEY AND CHILLI RISOTTO Bring stock and the water to the boil in medium saucepan. Reduce heat; simmer, covered. Heat oil in large saucepan; cook onion, stirring, until softened. Add rice; stir to coat in onion mixture. Add wine; cook, stirring, until liquid is absorbed. Stir in 1 cup simmering stock mixture; cook, stirring, over low heat until liquid is absorbed. Continue adding stock mixture, in 1-cup batches, stirring, until liquid is almost absorbed after each addition. Total cooking time should be about 35 minutes or until rice is tender. Just before serving, stir in rind, chilli, cheese and parsley; season to taste.

NUTRITIONAL COUNT PER SERVING 28.5g total fat (11g saturated fat); 2713kJ (649 cal); 63.3g carbohydrate; 29.7g protein; 3.1g fibre

ROASTED ROOT VEGETABLES

PREP + COOK TIME 1 HOUR SERVES 4

2 tablespoons olive oil
12 baby carrots (240g), peeled, halved lengthways
3 small parsnips (180g), peeled, quartered lengthways
12 baby new potatoes (480g), halved
4 baby onions (100g), halved 1 clove garlic, crushed
1 tablespoon coarsely chopped fresh rosemary
1 tablespoon honey 2 teaspoons seeded mustard
1 tablespoon lemon juice

1 Preheat oven to 220°C/425°F.
2 Heat oil in large flameproof baking dish; cook carrot, parsnip, potato and onion, stirring over heat, until browned lightly. Remove from heat; stir in garlic, rosemary, honey and mustard. Season.
3 Roast vegetables, in oven, uncovered, about 25 minutes or until vegetables are tender. Serve drizzled with lemon juice.
NUTRITIONAL COUNT PER SERVING 4.9g total fat (0.6g saturated fat); 798kJ (191 cal); 29.3g carbohydrate; 4.5g protein; 5.3g fibre

ROASTED BABY CARROTS WITH GARLIC

PREP + COOK TIME 35 MINUTES SERVES 10

3 bunches baby carrots (1kg) ¼ cup (60ml) olive oil
2 cloves garlic, crushed 2 teaspoons honey
1 tablespoon fresh thyme leaves

1 Preheat oven to 220°C/425°F.
2 Trim carrot tops, leaving 2cm (¾ inch) of the stems intact. Wash carrots well.
3 Place carrots in medium baking dish with combined oil, garlic and honey, season; toss well. Roast, uncovered, 15 minutes.
4 Add thyme leaves, roast a further 3 minutes or until carrots are tender.
NUTRITIONAL COUNT PER SERVING 5.6g total fat (0.8g saturated fat); 343kJ (82 cal); 6g carbohydrate; 0.7g protein; 3g fibre

Enjoy this succulent corn . . . Birds Eye Whole Kernel Corn . . . fresh, young, plump and juicy.

You'll love the natural flavour and freshness sealed in by Birds Eye miracle quick-freezing

Just taste the difference between delicious Birds Eye peas and ordinary peas in pods which have loitered from farm to market, to shop, to you. It's amazing! That's because Birds Eye peas are picked at their dewy best and quick-frozen *within two hours*. All their colour and flavour is sealed in and held, right to your table.

Back again! Sweet, young Birds Eye Peas
— peas that really taste "fresh from the garden"

SHELLED, WASHED, READY TO COOK

Now YOU CAN again enjoy really fresh peas — snatched from the pods at the moment of perfect sweetness, colour and tenderness, then shelled and quick-frozen so fast by Birds Eye, that all the sweet flavour and goodness is sealed in.

You save work and time. No tedious shelling — simply pop the peas straight into the pot. Birds Eye peas are so young and tender, they cook in only half the time. Let Birds Eye show you the way to buy peas *really fresh*, sweet — and already shelled, into the bargain.

You get full value. You don't pay for yellowish, starchy old peas — or wasteful pods. Birds Eye select only the pick of the crop. Every pea in the Birds Eye packet is perfect — lush green, tender, sweet.

BIRDS EYE *QUICK-FROZEN* **GREEN PEAS**

12 OZ. PACKET EQUALS 2 LB. PEAS IN THE POD — SERVES 6

If a packet of Birds Eye peas is more than you need for a meal, a sharp tap will divide the frozen peas. Neat!

········ Recipe ··················

MAKE YOUR DESSERTS MORE

DELICIOUS THAN EVER — WITH

BIRDS EYE ORCHARD-FRESH FRUITS!

Whipped up in minutes — a delicious dessert of fresh, sun-ripened *Birds Eye Peaches*, peeled, sliced, packed in pure syrup. Pile into glass sweet-dishes, top with a swirl of whipped cream or ice cream and a sprinkle of chopped nuts.
Try Birds Eye fresh *Raspberries* served, perhaps, in a rich butterscotch sauce — *Loganberries* baked in a tender pie-crust — or Birds Eye fresh *Tropical Fruit Salad* (tree-ripened bananas, passionfruit, pineapple, pawpaws) served very cold in a tall glass, garnished with mint. What a difference *really fresh* fruit makes!

BE 46. WWFPC

10

SINFULLY SWEET

IN AN ERA WHEN CALORIES WEREN'T COUNTED, DESSERTS AND PUDDINGS FLOURISHED. BECAUSE THE MAJORITY OF WOMEN DID NOT WORK, THEY WERE WELL VERSED IN THE ART OF BAKING AND DESSERT-MAKING; THEY SPENT HOURS IN THE KITCHEN CREATING THE WONDERFUL PIES, MERINGUES, JELLIES AND CAKES THAT WERE SO SYNONYMOUS WITH THE TIMES. MANY OF THESE RECIPES HAVE BEEN PASSED DOWN THE GENERATIONS AND LIVE ON TODAY AS FAMILY TRADITIONS.

BISCOTTEN TORTE

PREP TIME **1 HOUR (+ REFRIGERATION)** SERVES 8

24 Milk Coffee biscuits
½ cup (125ml) milk
1½ tablespoons rum
1¼ cup (310ml) thickened (heavy) cream
ALMOND FILLING
2 eggs, separated
125g (4 ounces) butter, chopped coarsely, softened
½ cup (110g) caster (superfine) sugar
few drops almond essence
1 cup (120g) ground almonds
½ cup (125ml) milk

1 Make almond filling.
2 Arrange six biscuits lengthways, in two rows of three each, on a large sheet of aluminium foil; brush biscuits generously with combined milk and rum. Spread biscuits with one-third of the almond filling. Repeat layering with remaining biscuits, milk and rum mixture, and almond filling, ending with a layer of biscuits. Wrap torte in foil; refrigerate 8 hours or overnight.
3 Beat cream in small bowl with electric mixer until soft peaks form. Cover torte with cream, running a fork lightly through the cream for a swirled effect. Top with fresh strawberries, if you like.
ALMOND FILLING Beat egg whites in small bowl with electric mixer until soft peaks form. Beat butter, sugar, essence and egg yolks in medium bowl with electric mixer until just combined; do not overmix. Stir in ground almonds; gradually beat in milk. Fold egg white into almond mixture.
NUTRITIONAL COUNT PER SERVING 42.9g total fat (22g saturated fat); 2186kJ (523 cal); 38.4g carbohydrate; 8.6g protein; 1.9g fibre
TIP It is fine to use just one 300ml carton of cream for this recipe.

CLASSIC RETRO RECIPE

CLASSIC TRIFLE

85g (3 ounces) raspberry jelly crystals

250g (8-ounce) sponge cake, cut into
  2.5cm (1-inch) pieces

¼ cup (60ml) sweet sherry

¼ cup (30g) custard powder

¼ cup (55g) caster (superfine) sugar

½ teaspoon vanilla extract

1½ cups (375ml) milk

825g (1¾ pounds) canned sliced peaches,
  drained

2⅓ cups (580ml) thickened (heavy) cream

1 Make jelly according to directions on packet; pour into shallow container. Refrigerate 20 minutes or until jelly is almost set.

2 Arrange cake in 3-litre (12-cup) bowl; sprinkle over sherry.

3 Blend custard powder, sugar and extract with a little of the milk in small saucepan; stir in remaining milk. Stir over heat until mixture boils and thickens. Cover surface of custard with plastic wrap; cool.

4 Pour jelly over cake; refrigerate 15 minutes. Top with peaches. Stir ⅓ cup of the cream into custard; pour over peaches.

5 Whip remaining cream; spread half over custard. Spoon remaining whipped cream into piping bag fitted with large fluted tube; pipe over top of trifle. Refrigerate 3 hours or overnight. Serve trifle topped with maraschino cherries, if you like.

NUTRITIONAL COUNT PER SERVING 31.4g total fat
(20.1g saturated fat); 1998kJ (478 cal);
48.7g carbohydrate; 6.4g protein; 1.5g fibre

TIP It is fine to use two 300ml (or one 600ml) cartons of cream for this recipe, so as not to waste the remaining 20ml.

RICE PUDDING WITH CARDAMOM AND RAISINS

PREP + COOK TIME 40 MINUTES   SERVES 4

1 litre (4 cups) milk
1¼ cups (310ml) pouring cream
1 cup (200g) arborio rice
½ cup (110g) caster (superfine) sugar
40g (1½ ounces) butter
¼ cup (55g) firmly packed light brown sugar
2 medium apples (300g), peeled, cored, quartered
½ teaspoon each ground cinnamon and cardamom
¾ cup (110g) raisins

1 Stir milk, cream, rice and caster sugar in large saucepan over heat, without boiling, until sugar dissolves. Bring to the boil; reduce heat. Cook, stirring, about 20 minutes or until rice is tender.
2 Meanwhile, melt butter in small saucepan; stir in brown sugar and apples. Stir over low heat about 10 minutes or until sauce is thickened and apples are caramelised and tender.
3 Stir spices and raisins into rice mixture; cook, stirring, 5 minutes.
4 Serve rice pudding topped with apples.
NUTRITIONAL COUNT PER SERVING 51g total fat (33.4g saturated fat); 4193kJ (1003 cal); 120g carbohydrate; 14.1g protein; 2.7g fibre
TIPS It is fine to use just one 300ml carton of cream for this recipe. You can use any dried fruit in place of the raisins in this recipe such as dried apricot or peach.

COFFEE CREME CARAMELS

LEMON PANNA COTTA POTS

PREP + COOK TIME 50 MINUTES (+ REFRIGERATION) SERVES 6

¾ cup (165g) caster (superfine) sugar • ¾ cup (180ml) water
6 eggs • ⅓ cup (75g) caster (superfine) sugar, extra
2 tablespoons coffee-flavoured liqueur
1 tablespoon instant coffee granules
1 tablespoon water, extra • 1½ cups (375ml) milk
1¼ cups (310ml) thickened (heavy) cream

1 Preheat oven to 160°C/325°F.
2 Stir sugar and the water in medium saucepan over heat, without boiling, until sugar dissolves. Bring to the boil; boil, uncovered, without stirring, about 5 minutes or until mixture is golden brown. Pour evenly into six 1-cup (250ml) ovenproof dishes.
3 Whisk eggs and extra sugar together in medium bowl; stir in liqueur and combined coffee and extra water.
4 Bring milk and cream to the boil in medium saucepan. Remove from heat. Gradually whisk milk mixture into egg mixture; strain into jug.
5 Place dishes in baking dish; pour custard into dishes. Pour enough boiling water into baking dish to come halfway up sides of dishes.
6 Bake crème caramels about 30 minutes or until just set. Remove dishes from water; cool. Refrigerate overnight.
7 Turn crème caramels onto serving plates.
NUTRITIONAL COUNT PER SERVING 26.9g total fat (15.9g saturated fat); 1363kJ (326 cal); 48.1g carbohydrate; 10g protein; 0.1g fibre
TIP It is fine to use just one 300ml carton of cream for this recipe.

**PREP + COOK TIME 15 MINUTES
(+ COOLING & REFRIGERATION) SERVES 8**

1 litre (4 cups) thickened (heavy) cream
3 teaspoons gelatine
¾ cup (165g) caster (superfine) sugar
½ teaspoon vanilla extract
1 teaspoon finely grated lemon rind
2 tablespoons lemon juice

1 Grease eight ⅔-cup (160ml) plastic dariole moulds or teacups.
2 Stir cream, gelatine, sugar and extract in medium saucepan, over heat, without boiling, until gelatine and sugar dissolve.
3 Strain mixture into large jug; stir in rind and juice. Cool.
4 Pour mixture into moulds, cover; refrigerate 4 hours or overnight.
5 Serve lemon panna cotta in moulds.
NUTRITIONAL COUNT PER SERVING 46.5g total fat (30.6g saturated fat); 2182kJ (522 cal); 24.7g carbohydrate; 3.1g protein; 0g fibre
SERVING SUGGESTION Serve with fresh fruit such as berries or stone fruit.

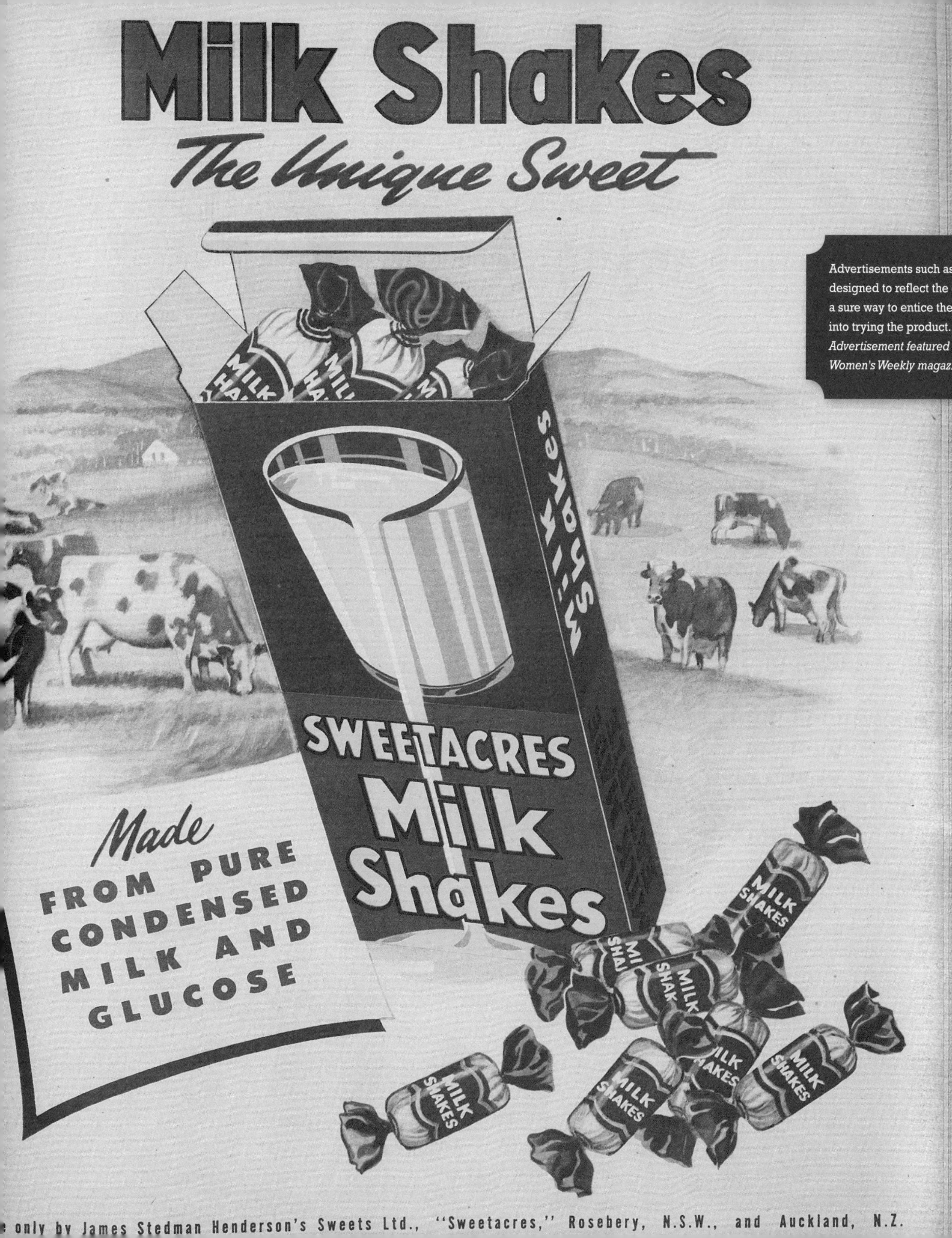

Milk Shakes
The Unique Sweet
MILK SHAKES
Milk Shakes
SWEETACRES
Milk
Shakes
Made
FROM PURE
CONDENSED
MILK AND
GLUCOSE
MILK SHAKES
MILK SHAKES
MILK SHAKES
MILK SHAKES
MILK SHAKES
e only by James Stedman Henderson's Sweets Ltd., "Sweetacres," Rosebery, N.S.W., and Auckland, N.Z.

Advertisements such as this one were designed to reflect the country life – a sure way to entice the city consumer into trying the product.
Advertisement featured in The Australian Women's Weekly magazine circa 1953

...LATE PUDDING

2 oz. sugar
cream
nuts

...der

...cocoa and sugar... a little cold milk, stir
... the milk to the boil.
... bring rema... mixture and return
... while stirring, to thic... a mould which has
... slow heat to thic... Leave to set. Turn out
...een rinsed with co... and nuts. In the picture
... and serve with wh... ing accompaniment. For
... tiny meringues ... o. 759.
... meringues see...

RICH CHARLOTTE RUSSE

544

¼ pint whipped cream
1 egg white
3 oz. sugar
¼ oz. gelatine
Savoy or sponge fingers

¼ pint sweet white wine
or mix white wine and
Maraschino
glacé cherries
silver balls

Pack a Charlotte mould or plain tin with the biscuits, so
that the round sides of the biscuits touch the side of the
mould and are quite close together. Beat the cream and
egg white until stiff. Dissolve the gelatine in the hot wine
or wine and Maraschino and mix in the sugar. Cool,
then stir into whipped cream. As soon as the mixture
starts to set fill the mould. Leave to set, turn out and tie
with a ribbon. The Charlotte is finally decorated with
whipped cream, cherries and silver balls.

LEMON CREAM MOULD

545

½ pint milk
juice of 2 lemons
grated rind of 1 lemon

3 oz. sugar
½ oz. gelatine*
½ gill water

* Enough to set 1 pint

Dissolve the gelatine with the sugar in the hot water.
Cool slightly and mix into the milk. Whisk in the lemon
juice and the grated lemon peel. As soon as the mixture
starts to set, pour into a mould, previously rinsed with
cold water. When set turn out and, if desired, decorate
with whipped cream and glacé fruit. If wished a few
drops of pink colouring can be added.

Original recipes and photographs from
the iconic *The Australian Women's Weekly
Cookery In Colour*, published in 1960
by *The Australian Women's Weekly* in
conjunction with Paul Hamlyn, London.

HOME-MADE ICE CREAM
in a refrigerator

546

It is not difficult to make ice cream at home, and while the excellent commercial products can be used when available, there may be occasions when you like to make your own.

Remember:

1) Use a good recipe, i.e. one with sufficient fat content. This is obtained by using canned or fresh cream, sweetened condensed milk or evaporated milk.

2) With most recipes it is advisable to freeze very quickly, so turn the indicator to the coldest position before starting to freeze the mixture.

3) With most recipes it is advisable to beat at least once, to give a light texture.

4) When ice cream has frozen, return indicator to normal position.

ONE-WHIP ICE CREAM
with gelatine

547

1 large can evaporated milk	1 teaspoon gelatine
	1 tablespoon boiling water
3 tablespoons castor sugar	1 teaspoon vanilla essence

Pour the undiluted evaporated milk, mixed with sugar, and gelatine dissolved in hot water, into the freezing tray. Chill until mixture starts to freeze round the edge. Pour into cold bowl, add vanilla and whisk sharply, until thick creamy consistency. Return to freezing tray until firm.

ICE CREAM MADE WITH EVAPORATED AND CONDENSED MILK

548

1 small can sweetened condensed milk	¼ pint water flavouring
½ pint evaporated milk	

Chill the condensed milk with the water. Whip the evaporated milk until thick. Fold into the condensed milk, add flavouring (see Recipe No. 551). Freeze until thick, turn into bowl and beat until very smooth. Replace in the trays and freeze again.

Although this recipe can be frozen very quickly, it does not matter so much; in fact you can freeze with the indicator in the normal storage setting.

STRAWBERRY ICE CREAM

549

Follow recipe No. 547 above, but instead of vanilla essence fold in ¼ pint strawberry purée — made from fresh, or well drained frozen or canned strawberries. This should be put in when beating in the bowl.

CREAM ICE

550

1 pint very well sweetened custard	2 small cans pure cream

Allow custard to cool, then add the cream. Freeze Recipe No. 549 above.

ICE CREAM FLAVOURINGS

551

1) Dissolve 1½ dessertspoons soluble coffee in the water in Recipe No. 548 or add to the custard in Recipe No. 550.

2) Melt 4 oz. plain chocolate with the ¼ pint in Recipe No. 548 or add to the custard No. 548 No. 550.

3) Stir ¼ pint thick fruit purée to either or No. 550

4) Use less sugar and add 4 oz. jam Recipe No. 548 or No. 550

QUINCE AND RHUBARB PIE

PREP + COOK TIME 3 HOURS (+ COOLING & REFRIGERATION)
SERVES 8

2 cups (500ml) water
2 cups (440g) caster (superfine) sugar
4 medium quinces (1.2kg), peeled, quartered
2 strips lemon rind
500g (1 pound) rhubarb, chopped coarsely
¼ cup (60ml) lemon juice, approximately
1 cup (150g) plain (all-purpose) flour
⅓ cup (55g) icing (confectioners') sugar
100g (3 ounces) cold butter, chopped coarsely
1 egg, separated
1 tablespoon iced water, approximately
1 tablespoon raw sugar

1 Stir the water and caster sugar in medium saucepan, over heat, without boiling, until sugar dissolves. Add quince and rind; bring to the boil. Reduce heat; simmer, covered, about 2 hours, or until quince is tender and a rosy colour. Add rhubarb; cook 5 minutes or until rhubarb softens. Add juice to taste, to reduce sweetness. Cool quince and rhubarb in the syrup.
2 Meanwhile, process flour, icing sugar and butter until crumbly. Add egg yolk and iced water, process until ingredients just come together. Knead gently on floured surface until smooth. Cover; refrigerate 30 minutes.
3 Preheat oven to 180°C/350°F. Grease 22cm (9-inch) pie dish.
4 Drain fruit mixture, reserving ⅓ cup of the syrup. Spoon fruit mixture and reserved syrup into dish.
5 Roll out pastry until large enough to cover pie. Cut 1cm (½-inch) rounds from pastry, reserving rounds. Place pastry over filling, trim edge with a knife. Place rounds on pastry, brush a little of the lightly beaten egg white over pastry; sprinkle with raw sugar. Place pie on an oven tray.
6 Bake pie about 30 minutes or until well browned. (Cover the edges of the pastry with foil after 20 minutes to prevent over-browning). Stand 10 minutes before serving with double (thick) cream, if you like.
NUTRITIONAL COUNT PER SERVING 11.6g total fat (7g saturated fat); 2061kJ (493 cal); 90.2g carbohydrate; 4.6g protein; 9.9g fibre

CHOCOLATE GANACHE MERINGUE

PREP + COOK TIME 1 HOUR 25 MINUTES (+ COOLING & REFRIGERATION) SERVES 8

3 egg whites

¾ cup (165g) caster (superfine) sugar

1 tablespoon cocoa powder

1½ cups (375ml) thickened (heavy) cream

1 tablespoon icing (confectioners') sugar

1 teaspoon vanilla extract

2 teaspoons cocoa powder, extra

GANACHE

100g (3 ounces) dark eating (semi-sweet) chocolate,
chopped coarsely

½ cup (125ml) thickened (heavy) cream

1 Preheat oven to 120°C/250°F. Draw one 8cm x 25cm (3¼-inch x 10-inch) rectangle on each of three pieces of baking paper. Place paper, upside down, on three oven trays.

2 Beat egg whites in small bowl with electric mixer until soft peaks form; gradually add caster sugar, beating until sugar dissolves. Fold in sifted cocoa powder.

3 Spread mixture evenly over rectangles. Bake about 45 minutes or until firm. Cool in oven with door ajar.

4 Make ganache.

5 Meanwhile, beat cream, icing sugar and extract in small bowl with electric mixer until soft peaks form.

6 Place one meringue layer on serving plate; spread with half the ganache, top with half the whipped cream. Place another meringue layer on top of the cream; repeat layers with remaining ganache and cream. Top with remaining meringue layer; dust with extra sifted cocoa powder.

GANACHE Stir ingredients in small saucepan over low heat until smooth. Refrigerate until almost firm.

NUTRITIONAL COUNT PER SERVING 27.2g total fat (18.9g saturated fat); 1246kJ (298 cal); 31.5g carbohydrate; 3.4g protein; 0.6g fibre

TIPS Make sure you turn the marked baking paper over so the markings don't transfer onto the meringues.

Meringue layers can be made four days ahead. Store in an airtight container in a cool, dry place. Assemble the meringue up to six hours before serving.

CHOCOLATE RASPBERRY TART

PREP + COOK TIME 50 MINUTES (+ REFRIGERATION & COOLING) SERVES 12

¾ cup (240g) raspberry jam
200g (6½ ounces) dark eating (semi-sweet) chocolate, chopped finely
25g (¾ ounce) unsalted butter, melted
⅔ cup (160ml) pouring cream, heated
125g (4 ounces) raspberries

SWEET PASTRY
1¼ cups (185g) plain (all-purpose) flour
½ cup (80g) icing (confectioners') sugar
125g (4 ounces) cold unsalted butter, chopped coarsely
¼ cup (60ml) iced water, approximately

1 Make sweet pastry.
2 Grease 12.5cm x 35cm (5-inch x 14-inch) loose-based flan tin. Roll pastry between sheets of baking paper until large enough to line tin. Ease pastry into tin, press into base and sides; trim edges, prick base with fork. Cover; refrigerate 30 minutes.
3 Preheat oven to 200°C/400°F.
4 Place tin on oven tray; cover pastry with baking paper, fill with dried beans or rice. Bake 15 minutes; remove paper and beans carefully. Bake pastry case about 10 minutes. Spread jam over pastry base; return to oven for 2 minutes. Cool.
5 Combine chocolate, melted butter and hot cream in medium bowl; whisk until smooth. Pour chocolate mixture into pastry case; refrigerate 2 hours. Top tart with raspberries.

SWEET PASTRY Process flour, icing sugar and butter until crumbly; with motor operating, add enough of the water until ingredients come together. Turn dough onto floured surface; knead gently until smooth. Wrap pastry in plastic; refrigerate 30 minutes.

NUTRITIONAL COUNT PER SERVING 21g total fat (13.4g saturated fat); 1559kJ (373 cal); 42.4g carbohydrate; 3g protein; 1.6g fibre

TIP YOU COULD ALSO
MAKE THIS TART IN FOUR
10CM (4-INCH) ROUND
LOOSE-BASED FLAN TINS.

GINGER AND ORANGE CAKES

MOCHA, PEAR AND NUT SELF-SAUCING PUDDINGS

PREP + COOK TIME 45 MINUTES (+ STANDING) MAKES 8

²/₃ cup (100g) plain (all-purpose) flour
²/₃ cup (100g) self-raising flour
½ teaspoon bicarbonate of soda (baking soda)
2 teaspoons each ground cinnamon and ginger
½ teaspoon ground cloves
1 cup (220g) firmly packed light brown sugar
²/₃ cup (160ml) buttermilk • 2 eggs, beaten lightly
100g (3 ounces) unsalted butter, melted

ORANGE GLAZE

1 cup (160g) icing (confectioners') sugar, sifted
½ teaspoon finely grated orange rind
1 tablespoon strained orange juice • 2 teaspoons hot water

1 Preheat oven to 180°C/350°F. Grease and flour eight holes of two 6-hole (¾-cup/180ml) mini fluted tube pans.
2 Sift flours, soda, spices and sugar into medium bowl; stir in buttermilk, eggs and butter. Divide mixture into pan holes; bake about 30 minutes. Turn cakes immediately onto greased wire rack over tray. Cool.
3 Make orange glaze. Pour glaze over cakes; stand until glaze is set.
ORANGE GLAZE Stir ingredients in medium bowl until smooth.
NUTRITIONAL COUNT PER CAKE 12.6g total fat (7.6g saturated fat); 1639kJ (392 cal); 65.8g carbohydrate; 5.5g protein; 1g fibre

PREP + COOK TIME 1 HOUR 10 MINUTES SERVES 8

2 medium pears (460g), sliced thinly
100g (3 ounces) dark eating (semi-sweet) chocolate, chopped
150g (4½ ounces) butter • ²/₃ cup (160ml) milk
1½ tablespoons instant coffee granules
²/₃ cup (70g) ground hazelnuts
¾ cup (165g) firmly packed light brown sugar
1 cup (150g) self-raising flour • 1 egg • 1¾ cups (430ml) water
¾ cup (165g) firmly packed light brown sugar, extra
½ cup (50g) cocoa powder

1 Preheat oven to 180°C/350°F. Grease eight 1¼-cup (310ml) ovenproof dishes. Place pear slices, slightly overlapping, in dishes.
2 Stir chocolate, 50g (1½ ounces) of the butter, milk and coffee in small saucepan over low heat until smooth. Transfer to large bowl; stir in ground hazelnuts and sugar, then sifted flour and egg. Pour over pear.
3 Stir the water, extra sugar, sifted cocoa and remaining butter in small saucepan over low heat until smooth. Slowly pour cocoa mixture over the back of a spoon onto pudding mixture.
4 Bake 30 minutes or until centre is firm; stand 5 minutes before serving.
NUTRITIONAL COUNT PER SERVING 27.1g total fat (15.1g saturated fat); 2266kJ (542 cal); 69.2g carbohydrate; 6.8g protein; 3.4g fibre

COTTEE'S REAL FRUIT JELLIES
WITH THE *Locked in* FLAVOUR

Jelly was a staple family dessert and manufacturers vied for a point of difference – this one, for example, is said to feature 'fragments' of real fruit. *Advertisement featured in The Australian Women's Weekly magazine circa 1953*

Cottee's STRAWBERRY FRUIT JELLY TABLET

Cottee's STRAWBERRY FRUIT JELLY TABLET "SEE THE FRUIT IN IT"

Strawberry Fruit Mould is fun to make and luscious to eat! Make up 1 packet of Cottee's Strawberry Jelly, as directed. Pour some of jelly (to a depth of about 1") in a wetted mould. When cool, but not set, arrange slices of peaches (or fruit in season) in this jelly and allow to set.

Here in each individually sealed cellophane cube is the real flavour of plump red strawberries . . . LOCKED IN until you are ready to release it! You'll actually see the fragments of strawberries as you savour the tantalising, fresh-fruit aroma. Once you've tried any of these Cottee's real fruit jellies, you'll never, never be content with any other STRAWBERRY, FRUIT SALAD, ORANGE, RASPBERRY, PINEAPPLE and a special favourite, LIME COOLA — they are all delicious.

Snow Tops are exciting and so easy. Make up a packet of Cottee's Lime Coola Jelly. Divide in two. Pour half into serving dishes to set and let the remainder stand until cold and beginning to "jell." Stir in one well-mashed ripe banana. Whip till thick and frothy and pile onto plain jelly. Chill before you serve—then watch the smiles.

Jelly Gems are real favourites. Make up two packets of Cottee's Jellies (different flavours). When set, chop into small particles and arrange in serving dishes. Top with cream or custard.

Strawberry Ice Cream. Combine in a small saucepan ½ a Cottee's Strawberry Jelly, 2 tablespoons sugar, ⅓ measuring cup hot or cold water. Stir over a moderate heat till dissolved. Stir in ⅔ measuring cup Cottee's Strawberry Topping and a rounded teaspoon thinly grated lemon rind. Chill 1½ measuring cups Carnation Milk till ice crystals form. Whip till thick and fluffy with rotary beater or electric mixer. Beat in the cooled jelly mixture. Freeze quickly till firm.

Cottee's REAL FRUIT JELLIES

BY THE MAKERS OF THE WORLD-FAMOUS PASSIONA

POLENTA AND ALMOND ORANGE CAKE

PREP + COOK TIME **2 HOURS 45 MINUTES (+ COOLING)** SERVES 12

2 medium oranges (480g)
²⁄₃ cup (110g) roasted blanched almonds
¾ cup (165g) caster (superfine) sugar
1 teaspoon baking powder
6 eggs
1 cup (120g) ground almonds
1 cup (170g) polenta
50g (1½ ounces) butter, melted

1 Cover unpeeled whole oranges in medium saucepan with cold water; bring to the boil. Boil, uncovered, 30 minutes; drain. Repeat process with fresh water, boil about 1 hour or until oranges are tender; drain. Cool oranges.

2 Preheat oven to 200°C/400°F. Grease deep 22cm (9-inch) round cake pan; line base and side with baking paper.

3 Blend or process blanched almonds with 1 tablespoon of the sugar until coarse.

4 Trim ends from oranges then cut in half; discard seeds. Blend or process oranges, including rind, with baking powder until mixture is pulpy.

5 Beat eggs with remaining sugar in small bowl with electric mixer until light and fluffy. Transfer to large bowl; fold in nut mixture, ground almonds, polenta, butter and orange pulp. Spread mixture into pan.

6 Bake cake about 50 minutes. Stand cake 5 minutes in pan before turning, top-side up, onto serving plate. Serve dusted with sifted icing (confectioners') sugar, if you like.

NUTRITIONAL COUNT PER SERVING 17g total fat (3.8g saturated fat); 1271kJ (304 cal); 27.8g carbohydrate; 8.8g protein; 2.9g fibre

Mr. and Mr

Every day Jerry return with another load exciting loot.

Illustration featured in *The Australian Women's Weekly* magazine, circa 1953

BLACK FOREST SOUFFLES

PREP + COOK TIME **40 MINUTES (+ COOLING)** SERVES **6**

⅔ cup (150g) caster (superfine) sugar
400g (12½ ounces) cherries, seeded, halved
2 tablespoons kirsch • 1 tablespoon lemon juice
50g (1½ ounces) butter • 1 tablespoon cocoa powder
½ cup (125ml) buttermilk • 125g (4 ounces) dark eating (semi-sweet) chocolate, chopped • 2 egg yolks • 4 egg whites

1 Preheat oven to 220°C/425°F. Grease six ¾-cup (180ml) soufflé dishes. Sprinkle inside of dishes with 1 tablespoon of the sugar; shake away excess. Place dishes on oven tray.
2 Stir cherries, kirsch, juice and ⅓ cup of the sugar in small saucepan over heat, without boiling, until sugar dissolves. Simmer, uncovered, without stirring, about 10 minutes or until mixture is syrupy. Cool.
3 Meanwhile, melt butter in small saucepan; stir in cocoa until smooth. Stir in buttermilk, heat without boiling. Remove from heat; stir in chocolate and 1½ tablespoons of the remaining sugar until smooth. Transfer mixture to large bowl; stir in egg yolks.
4 Beat egg whites in small bowl with electric mixer until soft peaks form; gradually add remaining sugar, beating until sugar dissolves. Fold egg white mixture into chocolate mixture, in two batches.
5 Divide cherry mixture among dishes; top with chocolate mixture.
6 Bake soufflés about 12 minutes or until puffed. Serve immediately.
NUTRITIONAL COUNT PER SERVING 15.8g total fat (11.3g saturated fat); 1246kJ (298 cal); 50.6g carbohydrate; 6.2g protein; 2.2g fibre

SPARKLING STONE FRUIT AND RASPBERRY JELLY

PREP + COOK TIME **25 MINUTES (+ REFRIGERATION)** SERVES **6**

½ cup (110g) caster (superfine) sugar
3 cups (750ml) sweet sparkling wine
1½ tablespoons gelatine • ½ cup (125ml) water
2 tablespoons lemon juice
1 medium nectarine (170g), sliced thinly
2 medium apricots (100g), sliced thinly
1 medium plum (110g), sliced thinly
200g (6½ ounces) raspberries

1 Stir sugar and 1 cup of the wine in medium saucepan over heat, without boiling, until sugar dissolves; bring to the boil. Reduce heat; simmer, uncovered, without stirring, 5 minutes.
2 Meanwhile, sprinkle gelatine over the water in small heatproof jug. Stand jug in small saucepan of simmering water; stir until gelatine dissolves. Stir gelatine mixture, remaining wine and juice into wine mixture; transfer mixture to heatproof jug.
3 Divide fruit among six 1-cup (250ml) serving glasses. Pour wine mixture over fruit. Cover; refrigerate 3 hours or overnight until firm.
NUTRITIONAL COUNT PER SERVING 0.2g total fat (0g saturated fat); 815kJ (195 cal); 25.8g carbohydrate; 3.7g protein; 3g fibre

CHOCOLATE MOUSSE PUFFS

PREP + COOK TIME 1 HOUR (+ REFRIGERATION) MAKES 32

1 cup (250ml) water
80g (2½ ounces) butter, chopped coarsely
1 cup (150g) plain (all-purpose) flour
2 tablespoons cocoa powder
4 eggs

CHOCOLATE MOUSSE FILLING
125g (4 ounces) cream cheese, softened
⅔ cup (150g) caster (superfine) sugar
2 egg yolks
1⅔ cups (250g) white chocolate melts, melted
2⅔ cups (580ml) thickened (heavy) cream, whipped

1 Make chocolate mousse filling.

2 Preheat oven to 220°C/425°F. Grease oven trays.

3 Bring the water and butter to the boil in medium saucepan. Add sifted flour and cocoa; beat with wooden spoon over heat until mixture comes away from base and side of pan and forms a smooth ball.

4 Transfer mixture to small bowl; beat in eggs, one at a time, with electric mixer until mixture is thick and glossy. Drop level tablespoons of mixture, about 5cm (2 inches) apart, on trays; bake 15 minutes. Reduce oven to 200°C/400°F.

5 Split puffs in half, use a teaspoon to scoop out any uncooked mixture; return halves, cut-side up, to oven trays.

6 Bake puffs about 10 minutes or until puffs are crisp; cool on wire racks.

7 Spoon mousse filling into half of the puffs, replace tops. Serve dusted with extra sifted cocoa powder or drinking chocolate.

CHOCOLATE MOUSSE FILLING Beat cheese, sugar and egg yolks in large bowl with electric mixer until smooth. Just before melted chocolate sets, beat into cheese mixture then fold in cream, in two batches. Cover; refrigerate until cold.

NUTRITIONAL COUNT PER PUFF 13.8g total fat (8.6g saturated fat); 694kJ (166 cal); 12.9g carbohydrate; 2.9g protein; 0.2g fibre

TIPS It is fine to use two 300ml (or one 600ml) cartons of cream for this recipe, so as not to waste the remaining 20ml.
Unfilled puffs and chocolate mousse filling can be made a day ahead; assemble just before serving.

CHOCOLATE GANACHE AND RASPBERRY CAKE

PREP + COOK TIME 1 HOUR 50 MINUTES (+ STANDING)   SERVES 12

⅓ cup (35g) cocoa powder

⅓ cup (80ml) water

150g (4½ ounces) dark eating (semi-sweet) chocolate, melted

150g (4½ ounces) butter, melted

1⅓ cups (300g) firmly packed light brown sugar

1 cup (120g) ground almonds

4 eggs, separated

300g (9½ ounces) raspberries

GANACHE

200g (6½ ounces) dark eating (semi-sweet) chocolate, chopped coarsely

⅔ cup (160ml) thickened (heavy) cream

1 Preheat oven to 160°C/325°F. Grease deep 22cm (9-inch) round cake pan; line base and side with baking paper.

2 Blend sifted cocoa powder with the water in large bowl until smooth; stir in chocolate, butter, sugar, ground almonds and egg yolks.

3 Beat egg whites in small bowl with electric mixer until soft peaks form; fold into chocolate mixture, in two batches. Pour mixture into pan.

4 Bake cake about 1¼ hours. Stand cake in pan 15 minutes before turning, top-side up, onto wire rack to cool.

5 Make ganache.

6 Place raspberries on top of cake; drizzle ganache over raspberries. Stand cake at room temperature until chocolate sets.

GANACHE Stir ingredients in small saucepan over low heat until smooth.

NUTRITIONAL COUNT PER SERVING 31.8g total fat (19.2g saturated fat); 2027kJ (485 cal); 44g carbohydrate; 6.7g protein; 3.7g fibre

TIPS Undecorated cake is suitable to freeze. The cake can be made up to three days in advance; top cake with raspberries and chocolate on the day of serving.

11

HERE COMES SANTA

EXTRAVAGANCE IS ALWAYS THE ORDER OF THE DAY AT CHRISTMAS, BUT FIFTY YEARS AGO, PEOPLE OFTEN SAVED ALL YEAR FOR THE SPECIAL FEAST THAT WAS PREPARED ON CHRISTMAS DAY. POULTRY — CHICKEN, GOOSE OR TURKEY — MADE ITS ANNUAL APPEARANCE AND TRADITIONAL CHRISTMAS PUDDINGS AND CAKES, MADE MONTHS IN ADVANCE, TOOK PRIDE OF PLACE ON TABLES FESTOONED WITH DECORATIONS, BON BONS AND THE VERY BEST FAMILY CHINA.

ROAST TURKEY WITH FORCEMEAT STUFFING

PREP + COOK TIME 3 HOURS 45 MINUTES (+ COOLING & STANDING) SERVES 8

4.5kg (9-pound) whole turkey

1 cup (250ml) water

80g (2½ ounces) butter, melted

¼ cup (35g) plain (all-purpose) flour

3 cups (750ml) chicken stock

½ cup (125ml) dry white wine

FORCEMEAT STUFFING

40g (1½ ounces) butter

3 medium brown onions (450g), chopped finely

2 rindless bacon slices (130g), chopped coarsely

1 cup (70g) stale breadcrumbs

½ cup coarsely chopped fresh flat-leaf parsley

250g (8 ounces) minced (ground) pork

250g (8 ounces) minced (ground) chicken

1 Preheat oven to 180°C/350°F.

2 Make forcemeat stuffing.

3 Discard neck from turkey. Rinse turkey under cold water; pat dry inside and out with absorbent paper. Fill neck cavity loosely with forcemeat; secure skin over opening with small skewers. Fill large cavity loosely with forcemeat; tie legs together with kitchen string. Tuck wings under turkey.

4 Place turkey on oiled wire rack in large shallow flameproof baking dish; pour the water into dish. Brush turkey all over with half the butter; season. Cover turkey tightly with two layers of greased foil. Roast 2 hours.

5 Uncover turkey; brush with remaining butter. Roast turkey, uncovered, about 1 hour or until cooked through. Remove turkey from dish, cover loosely with foil; stand 20 minutes.

6 Pour juice from dish into large jug; skim 1 tablespoon of fat from juice, return fat to same dish. Skim and discard fat from remaining juice; reserve juice. Add flour to dish; cook, stirring, until mixture bubbles and is well-browned. Gradually stir in stock, wine and reserved juice; cook, stirring, until gravy boils and thickens. Strain gravy into jug; serve with turkey.

FORCEMEAT STUFFING Melt butter in medium frying pan; cook onion and bacon, stirring, over low heat, until onion softens. Cool. Combine onion mixture and remaining ingredients in large bowl; season.

NUTRITIONAL COUNT PER SERVING 56g total fat (21.5g saturated fat); 3724kJ (891 cal); 13.1g carbohydrate; 81.5g protein; 1.5g fibre

TIPS To test if the turkey is cooked, insert a skewer sideways into the thickest part of the thigh, then remove and press flesh to release the juices. If the juice runs clear, the turkey is cooked. Alternatively, insert a meat thermometer into the thickest part of the thigh, without touching the bone; the turkey is cooked when the thermometer reaches 90°C/195°F.

CLASSIC
RETRO
RECIPE

CLASSIC STEAMED CHRISTMAS PUDDING

PREP + COOK TIME 4 HOURS 30 MINUTES (+ STANDING) SERVES 12

1¾ cups (280g) sultanas

1 cup (160g) dried currants

1¼ cups (185g) raisins, chopped coarsely

1 cup (140g) seeded dried dates,
  chopped coarsely

1 cup (200g) dried figs, chopped coarsely

¼ cup (50g) red glacé cherries, quartered

½ cup (125g) glacé fruit (such as apricot,
  pineapple, peach), chopped coarsely

¾ cup (180ml) brandy, port or dark rum

200g (6½ ounces) butter, softened

1 cup (220g) firmly packed
  dark brown sugar

½ cup (180g) treacle or golden syrup

3 eggs

1¼ cups (185g) plain (all-purpose) flour

1 teaspoon each ground cinnamon,
  ginger and mixed spice

3 cups (210g) stale breadcrumbs

BRANDY CUSTARD

2 cups (500ml) milk

1¼ cups (310ml) pouring cream

1 vanilla bean, split lengthways

6 egg yolks

½ cup (110g) caster (superfine) sugar

2 tablespoons brandy

1 Combine fruit in large bowl. Heat brandy in small saucepan over medium heat until hot; do not boil. Remove from heat; pour over fruit, stir to combine. Cover; stand at room temperature for 24 hours or store in a cool, dark place for up to one week, stirring every day.

2 Grease 2-litre (8-cup) pudding basin or steamer. Line base with a round of baking paper. Place 30cm x 40cm (12-inch x 16-inch) sheet of foil on bench; top with baking paper cut the same size. Fold a 5cm (2-inch) pleat crossways through centre of both sheets.

3 Beat butter, sugar and treacle in small bowl with electric mixer until combined. Beat in eggs, one at a time. Mix butter mixture into fruit mixture; stir in sifted dry ingredients and breadcrumbs. Spoon mixture into basin. Top with pleated baking paper and foil (this allows pudding to expand as it cooks); secure with kitchen string or lid.

4 Place pudding in steamer with enough boiling water to come halfway up side of steamer. Cover with tight-fitting lid; boil 4 hours, replenishing with boiling water as necessary to maintain water level. Stand pudding 10 minutes before turning out.

5 Meanwhile, make brandy custard. Serve pudding with custard.

BRANDY CUSTARD Bring milk, cream and vanilla bean to the boil in medium saucepan. Remove from heat; stand 10 minutes. Discard vanilla bean. Beat egg yolks and sugar in medium bowl with electric mixer until thick and creamy; gradually beat in warm milk mixture. Return custard to pan; stir, over heat, without boiling, until custard is thick and coats the back of a spoon. Stir in brandy.

NUTRITIONAL COUNT PER SERVING 33.3g total fat (19.5g saturated fat); 3570kJ (854 cal); 126.4g carbohydrate; 12.6g protein; 7.7g fibre

TIP It is fine to use just one 300ml carton of cream in the brandy custard.

TO STORE Allow pudding to come to room temperature then wrap in plastic wrap; refrigerate in a clean steamer, or seal tightly in a freezer bag or airtight container. Refrigerate for up to two months; freeze for up to 12 months.

TO REHEAT Thaw frozen pudding for three days in refrigerator; remove from refrigerator 12 hours before reheating. Remove from plastic wrap and return to steamer. Steam 2 hours following instructions in step 4.

TO REHEAT IN MICROWAVE You can reheat up to four single serves at once. Cover with plastic wrap; microwave on HIGH (100%) up to 1 minute per serve. To reheat whole pudding, cover with plastic wrap; microwave on MEDIUM (55%) about 15 minutes or until heated through.

SEARED TUNA WITH VERJUICE DRESSING

PREP + COOK TIME 1 HOUR (+ REFRIGERATION) SERVES 6

2 tablespoons hot english mustard

¼ cup (60ml) light soy sauce

1 tablespoon peanut oil

800g (1½-pound) piece tuna fillet

6 eggs

8 baby new potatoes (320g), halved

250g (8 ounces) green beans, trimmed

1 cup (150g) seeded black olives

250g (8 ounces) cherry tomatoes, halved

1 small red onion (100g), cut into wedges

VERJUICE DRESSING

2 tablespoons verjuice

1 tablespoon dijon mustard

¼ cup (60ml) walnut oil

1 tablespoon finely chopped fresh chervil

1 Combine mustard, sauce, oil and tuna in large bowl. Cover; refrigerate 3 hours or overnight.

2 Boil eggs in medium saucepan of water about 4 minutes or until eggs are medium boiled. Cool, then peel and halve each egg.

3 Make verjuice dressing.

4 Boil, steam or microwave potato and beans, separately, until tender; drain. Place potato, beans, olives, tomato, onion and dressing in large bowl; toss gently to combine. Top with eggs; season to taste.

5 Remove tuna from marinade; discard marinade. Cook tuna on heated barbecue (or grill or grill plate) about 10 minutes, turning, until marked well on all sides and cooked to your liking. Remove from heat, cover loosely with foil; stand 10 minutes.

6 Cut tuna into slices; serve with salad.

VERJUICE DRESSING Place ingredients in screw-top jar; shake well.

NUTRITIONAL COUNT PER SERVING 25.7g total fat (6g saturated fat); 2006kJ (480 cal); 16.2g carbohydrate; 43.8g protein; 3.6g fibre

TIPS Verjuice is an unfermented grape juice with a fresh lemony-vinegar flavour. It's available from most supermarkets, usually in the vinegar section.

Buy individual tuna steaks instead of the fillet, if you prefer. Cook steaks for about 5 minutes; the time will depend on their thickness.

BAKED HAM WITH CRANBERRY AND REDCURRANT GLAZE

PREP + COOK TIME 1 HOUR 50 MINUTES (+ STANDING)   SERVES 12

8kg (16-pound) cooked leg of ham
whole cloves, to decorate
CRANBERRY AND REDCURRANT GLAZE
1 cup (320g) redcurrant jelly
¾ cup (240g) cranberry sauce
2 tablespoons lemon juice
⅓ cup (80ml) brandy

1 Preheat oven to 180°C/350°F.
2 Cut through the rind of the ham about 10cm (4 inches) from the shank end of the leg. To remove the rind, run your thumb around the edge of the rind, just under the skin. Start pulling the rind from the widest edge of the ham; continue to pull the rind carefully away from the fat up to the cut at the shank end. Remove rind completely. Using a sharp knife, score fat lightly at about 2.5cm (1-inch) intervals, cutting just through the surface of the fat. Score in the opposite direction to form a diamond pattern.
3 Make cranberry and redcurrant glaze.
4 Line large baking dish with baking paper; place ham on wire rack in dish. Brush ham all over with glaze; cover shank end with foil.
5 Bake ham 40 minutes; remove from oven, decorate with cloves. Return to oven; bake a further 40 minutes or until browned all over, brushing occasionally with glaze.
6 Cover ham; stand 15 minutes before slicing. Serve warm or cold.
CRANBERRY AND REDCURRANT GLAZE Stir ingredients in small saucepan over low heat until combined.
NUTRITIONAL COUNT PER SERVING 37.5g total fat (12.8g saturated fat); 3369kJ (806 cal); 26g carbohydrate; 88.5g protein; 0.4g fibre

ROAST BALSAMIC CHICKEN WITH GARLIC BREAD SAUCE

PREP + COOK TIME 1 HOUR 50 MINUTES (+ REFRIGERATION & STANDING)   SERVES 6

1.8kg (3½-pound) whole chicken

⅓ cup (80ml) balsamic vinegar

1 tablespoon dijon mustard

1 tablespoon olive oil

2 sprigs fresh rosemary

500g (1 pound) cherry truss tomatoes

2 sprigs fresh thyme

GARLIC BREAD SAUCE

4 cloves garlic, bruised

2 fresh bay leaves

1¾ cups (430ml) milk

1½ cups (110g) stale breadcrumbs

30g (1 ounce) butter

½ cup (125ml) pouring cream

1 Rinse chicken under cold water. Pat dry inside and out with absorbent paper. Combine vinegar, mustard and oil in large bowl, add chicken; turn to coat chicken in marinade. Cover; refrigerate 3 hours.

2 Preheat oven to 200°C/400°F.

3 Place chicken in large baking dish; reserve marinade. Place one rosemary sprig into chicken cavity. Tie legs together with kitchen string; season. Roast, uncovered, about 1½ hours or until cooked through, basting with reserved marinade. Add tomatoes to dish for last 10 minutes of cooking time.

4 Meanwhile, make garlic bread sauce.

5 Tuck remaining rosemary and thyme between drumsticks; serve chicken with sauce and tomatoes.

GARLIC BREAD SAUCE Bring garlic, bay leaves and milk to the boil in small saucepan. Remove from heat, stand 30 minutes. Strain milk mixture, discard solids; return milk mixture to same pan. Stir in breadcrumbs and butter; cook, stirring, over low heat, about 10 minutes or until thick. Add cream, stir until heated through; season to taste.

NUTRITIONAL COUNT PER SERVING 47g total fat (19g saturated fat); 2717kJ (650 cal); 19.9g carbohydrate; 36.3g protein; 2.6g fibre

ITALIAN-STYLE TURKEY ROLL WITH PORK AND FENNEL SAUSAGE STUFFING

PREP + COOK TIME 1 HOUR 30 MINUTES (+ COOLING) SERVES 12

1.5kg (3-pound) single turkey breast, skin on

1 tablespoon olive oil

6 baby fennel bulbs (780g), halved

1 medium lemon (140g), quartered

½ cup (125ml) dry white wine

PORK AND FENNEL SAUSAGE STUFFING

½ cup (35g) stale breadcrumbs

⅓ cup (80ml) milk

1 tablespoon olive oil

1 medium brown onion (150g), chopped finely

2 cloves garlic, crushed

70g (2½ ounces) rocket (arugula), chopped finely

7 pork and fennel sausages (560g), cases removed

1 Preheat oven to 200°C/400°F.

2 Make pork and fennel sausage stuffing.

3 Pat turkey dry with absorbent paper; place, skin-side down, on board. Starting from one long edge, slice through centre, horizontally, not quite through to the other side, to open out flat. Spread with stuffing. Roll turkey tightly to secure stuffing. Using kitchen string, tie into a neat roll at 2.5cm (1-inch) intervals.

4 Heat oil in large baking dish in oven 5 minutes. Add turkey roll; turn to coat in oil. Place fennel and lemon around turkey; add wine to dish. Roast, uncovered, about 50 minutes or until turkey is cooked through, basting turkey frequently.

5 Cover turkey loosely with foil; stand 10 minutes before slicing. Serve with fennel and lemon.

PORK AND FENNEL SAUSAGE STUFFING Combine breadcrumbs and milk in small bowl. Heat oil in medium frying pan; cook onion, stirring occasionally, until tender. Stir in garlic, then stir in rocket until wilted. Transfer to medium bowl; cool 20 minutes. Stir in sausage mince and breadcrumb mixture; season.

NUTRITIONAL COUNT PER SERVING 24.5g total fat (7.3g saturated fat); 1630kJ (390 cal); 6.8g carbohydrate; 32.8g protein; 3g fibre

TIPS It's important not to overcrowd the turkey, fennel and lemon in the baking dish so they cook evenly and caramelise. When the roll is cooked, juices should run clear when tested with a skewer.

CERTAIN SUCCESS WITH
PASTRY

ingredients, utensils and hands as cool as possible.

...ze bowl rather than a small basin for short
...that there is plenty of air space.

...ing fat into flour, lift hands as much as
...that air is introduced into dough.

...fat only with forefinger and thumb. Too much
...sure when rubbing in will make pastry too sticky.

5.   Sieve flour before mixing. This lightens the dough.

6.   It is undoubtedly better to use plain flour for all pastry.
     Many people however prefer self-raising flour for short
     pastry, especially when the proportion of fat is de-
     creased, so if successful with self-raising flour don't
     change. For richer pastry, i.e. flaky or puff pastry, it is
     better to use plain flour.

7.   The consistency of the dough is all-important. Be care-
     ful not to make it too wet, as this produces a hard
     pastry. If the dough it too dry, it will be difficult to roll
     out. Generally speaking the dough is the right texture
     when it rolls into a large ball, with very little handling.

8.   Pastry should be baked quickly.

9.   When using very hard fat (perhaps straight from the
     refrigerator) which is almost impossible to rub into the
     flour, you will find it helpful to grate it on a coarse
     grater or to soften it by working with a knife. When
     making flan pastry the fat can be slightly warmed first.

10. When making short pastry oil can be used instead of fat.
     For each ounce of fat substitute a scant tablespoon of oil.
     This will give the pastry a very crisp crust.

11. When rolling out pastry remember never to roll the
     rolling-pin backwards and forwards. It should roll one
     way only — straight ahead. The pastry should be
     turned at right angles to obtain right shape.

12. When rolling the pastry, lift rolling-pin from time to
     time. This helps to keep the dough light.

     ...recipe says that the pastry case should be baked
     ...blind' means empty. To prevent the bottom of the
     ...with crusts of stale bread or
     ...sed grease-proof paper
     ...five minutes before

561 CHOOSING FAT FOR PASTR...

There have been many developments in fats...
and so you will find with most of the basic rec...
of the fats you can use. Try them all — they...
excellent results and a slightly different taste a...
— so you can vary your pastry.

562 AMOUNT OF PASTRY IN...

When a recipe directs 'use 4 oz....
pastry (or puff)' it means pastry mad...
flour etc. — not a total weight of 4...

563   MERRY MINCE PIE...

1 lb. mincemeat   cinnamon...
3 eating apples   nutmeg...
3 oz. brown sugar   biscuit...
                         (Rec...

Roll out biscuit pie crust to ⅛ inch thi...
for individual pies. Then fold up...
⅛ inch thick, and cut out rounds to li...
pie shells with alternate layers of min...
sliced eating apple sprinkled with a...
and nutmeg. If cooking apples are use...
Cut out a 'star' from each pastry li...
with a little sugar. Bake in centre...
minutes. For a special occasion arra...
picture opposite.

Original recipes and photographs from
the iconic *The Australian Women's Weekly
Cookery In Colour*, published in 1960
by *The Australian Women's Weekly* in
conjunction with Paul Hamlyn, London.

ROAST PORK LOIN WITH CRANBERRY SAUCE

PREP + COOK TIME 2 HOURS (+ STANDING)   SERVES 8

2kg (4-pound) boneless loin of pork, rind on

60g (2 ounces) butter

1 tablespoon olive oil

1 medium red onion (170g), chopped finely

1 clove garlic, crushed

100g (3 ounces) mild salami, chopped finely

1 tablespoon finely chopped fresh sage

¼ cup (35g) pistachios, roasted

¼ cup (35g) dried cranberries

½ cup (35g) stale breadcrumbs

2 tablespoons fine table salt

½ cup (125ml) port

¼ cup (80g) cranberry sauce

1½ cups (375ml) chicken stock

ROASTED VEGETABLES

500g (1 pound) pumpkin, cut into wedges

2 medium parsnips (500g), quartered

2 medium red onions (340g), quartered

500g (1 pound) baby carrots, trimmed

12 baby new potatoes (480g), halved

¼ cup (60ml) olive oil

2 tablespoons fresh thyme leaves

1 Preheat oven to 200°C/400°F.

2 Using sharp knife, score pork skin by making shallow cuts at 1cm (½-inch) intervals. Place pork on board, fat-side down; slice through the thickest part of the pork horizontally, without cutting through the other side. Open pork out to form one large piece. Trim pork, reserving 150g (4½ ounces) of the pork trimmings; blend or process the trimmings with 20g (¾ ounce) of the butter; reserve for seasoning.

3 To make seasoning, heat oil in medium frying pan; cook onion and garlic, stirring, until onion softens. Add remaining butter, salami, sage, nuts and cranberries; cook, stirring, 2 minutes. Transfer mixture to medium bowl; cool. Stir in breadcrumbs then trimmings and butter mixture; season.

4 Press seasoning mixture along one long side of pork; roll pork to enclose filling. Secure with kitchen string at 2cm (¾-inch) intervals. Rub pork skin with salt; place on oiled wire rack in large shallow baking dish. Roast, uncovered, about 1¼ hours or until pork is cooked through.

5 Meanwhile, cook roasted vegetables.

6 Remove pork from dish; cover pork loosely with foil, stand 15 minutes. Drain excess fat from dish, add port, sauce and stock to dish; stir over heat until sauce is reduced by half. Season to taste; cover to keep warm.

7 Serve sliced pork with sauce and vegetables.

ROASTED VEGETABLES Combine vegetables in large baking dish with oil and thyme. Roast, uncovered, for last 30 minutes of pork cooking time, turning once. Season to taste.

NUTRITIONAL COUNT PER SERVING 27.3g total fat (8.9g saturated fat); 2801kJ (670 cal); 34.7g carbohydrate; 64.9g protein; 6.3g fibre

TIPS When you order the pork loin, ask your butcher to leave a flap measuring about 20cm (8 inches) in length to help make rolling the loin easier. For exceptional crackling, ensure pork skin is dry and well-seasoned with fine salt. Pat the pork dry with absorbent paper, then leave it in the fridge, uncovered, for a few hours or overnight so the skin dries out nicely before cooking.

CHERRY AND PISTACHIO TERRINE

PREP + COOK TIME 1 HOUR 25 MINUTES   SERVES 8

10 slices thin bacon (300g)

1 tablespoon olive oil

3 shallots (75g), chopped finely

1 clove garlic, crushed

1 tablespoon finely chopped fresh sage

250g (8 ounces) minced (ground) pork

250g (8 ounces) minced (ground) veal

1 egg, beaten lightly

½ cup (35g) stale breadcrumbs

⅓ cup (45g) pistachios, roasted

1 cup (150g) cherries, seeded

3 chicken tenderloins (225g)

1 tablespoon redcurrant jelly, warmed

CHERRY COMPOTE

⅓ cup (110g) redcurrant jelly

2 tablespoons port

1 cup (125g) coarsely chopped seeded cherries

1 Preheat oven to 180°C/350°F. Line medium shallow baking dish with baking paper.

2 Cut eye sections (the fat end) from the bacon; reserve for another use.

3 Heat oil in small frying pan; cook shallots and garlic, stirring, until shallot softens. Stir in sage.

4 Combine shallot mixture, pork, veal, egg and breadcrumbs in large bowl; season. Stir in nuts and cherries.

5 Shape half the pork mixture into an 8cm x 24cm (3¼-inch x 9½-inch) log in baking dish. Place chicken tenderloins lengthways down centre of pork mixture, then top with remaining pork mixture. Wrap bacon slices, overlapping slightly, around log; tuck ends under log. Pat into a neat round. Brush bacon with half the redcurrant jelly.

6 Bake terrine about 45 minutes or until cooked through, brushing with remaining redcurrant jelly halfway through cooking time.

7 Meanwhile, make cherry compote.

8 Serve terrine with cherry compote.

CHERRY COMPOTE Combine jelly and port in small saucepan; simmer, stirring, 3 minutes. Add cherries; cool.

NUTRITIONAL COUNT PER SERVING 21.4g total fat (6.7g saturated fat); 1639kJ (392 cal); 20.3g carbohydrate; 28.2g protein; 1.6g fibre

TIPS Some butchers sell a minced (ground) pork and veal mixture, this is fine to use here; you need to buy 500g (1 pound).
You can use cherry jam instead of the redcurrant jelly for the cherry compote.

FIG MINCE PIES

PREP + COOK TIME 1 HOUR 40 MINUTES (+ STANDING & REFRIGERATION) MAKES 24

150g (4½ ounces) dried figs, chopped finely

½ cup (65g) dried cranberries

½ cup (75g) raisins, chopped coarsely

¼ cup (40g) mixed peel

¼ cup (55g) finely chopped glacé ginger

¼ cup (60g) finely chopped glacé peach

1 medium apple (150g), peeled, grated

½ cup (110g) firmly packed light brown sugar

2 tablespoons fig jam

1 teaspoon finely grated orange rind

2 tablespoons orange juice

1 cinnamon stick, halved

1 teaspoon mixed spice

⅓ cup (80ml) brandy

1½ sheets shortcrust pastry

1 egg white, beaten lightly

PASTRY

2 cups (300g) plain (all-purpose) flour

⅓ cup (75g) caster (superfine) sugar

150g (4½ ounces) cold butter, chopped coarsely

1 egg, beaten lightly

1 Combine fruit, sugar, jam, rind, juice, spices and brandy in medium bowl. Cover; stand at room temperature for one week or up to a month, stirring mixture every two or three days.

2 Make pastry.

3 Grease two 12-hole (2-tablespoon/40ml) deep flat-based patty pans. Divide pastry in half; roll one portion of dough between sheets of baking paper to 3mm (⅛-inch) thickness; cut 12 x 7cm (2¾-inch) rounds from pastry. Repeat with remaining pastry. Press rounds into pan holes; prick bases all over with fork. Refrigerate 30 minutes.

4 Preheat oven to 200°C/400°F.

5 Cut whole shortcrust pastry sheet into 16 squares; cut each square into six strips. Cut the half pastry sheet into eight squares; cut each square into six strips.

6 Use six strips to make a lattice pattern. Cut a 6.5cm (2¾-inch) round from latticed pastry. Repeat with remaining pastry strips.

7 Discard cinnamon stick from fruit mince, spoon fruit mince into pastry cases; top with lattice pastry rounds. Press edges to seal; brush pastry with egg white.

8 Bake pies about 20 minutes. Dust with a little sifted icing (confectioners') sugar before serving, if you like.

PASTRY Process flour, sugar and butter until crumbly. Add egg; process until combined. Knead pastry on floured surface until smooth. Cover; refrigerate 30 minutes.

NUTRITIONAL COUNT PER SERVING 8.5g total fat (5g saturated fat); 936kJ (224 cal); 35.4g carbohydrate; 2.8g protein; 2.1g fibre

TIPS Mince pies will keep in an airtight container for up to two weeks. Make double the quantity of fruit mince to bottle for gifts.

Here Comes Santa

GOLDEN BOILED PUDDING

PREP + COOK TIME 3 HOURS 40 MINUTES (+ STANDING)   SERVES 16

1 cup (180g) finely chopped dried pears
1 cup (130g) finely chopped dried cranberries
1 cup (75g) finely chopped dried apples
½ cup (80g) finely chopped dried apricots
1 large apple (200g), peeled, grated coarsely
⅓ cup (80ml) orange-flavoured liqueur
2 teaspoons finely grated orange rind
2 tablespoons orange juice
250g (8 ounces) butter, softened
1½ cups (330g) caster (superfine) sugar
4 eggs
1 cup (150g) plain (all-purpose) flour
½ teaspoon bicarbonate of soda (baking soda)
1 teaspoon ground cinnamon
3 cups (210g) stale breadcrumbs
1 cup (120g) ground almonds
⅔ cup (100g) plain (all-purpose) flour, extra
60cm (24-inch) square unbleached calico (see tips)

1 Combine fruit, liqueur, rind and juice in large bowl. Cover, stand at room temperature overnight.

2 Beat butter and sugar in small bowl with electric mixer until combined; beat in eggs, one at a time. Mix butter mixture into fruit mixture. Mix in sifted flour, soda and cinnamon, then breadcrumbs and ground almonds.

3 Fill boiler three-quarters full of hot water, cover with tight-fitting lid; bring to the boil. Have ready 1-metre (1-yard) length of kitchen string and extra plain flour. Wearing thick rubber gloves, dip pudding cloth into boiling water. Boil 1 minute then remove; squeeze excess water from cloth. Quickly spread hot cloth on bench. Rub extra flour into centre of cloth to cover an area about 40cm (16 inches) in diameter, leaving flour a little thicker in centre of cloth where "skin" on pudding needs to be thickest.

4 Place pudding mixture in centre of cloth. Gather cloth evenly around mixture, avoiding any deep pleats; pat into round shape. Tie cloth tightly with string as close to mixture as possible. Pull ends of cloth tightly to ensure pudding is as round and as firm as possible; tie loops in string.

5 Lower pudding into the boiling water; tie ends of string to handles of boiler to suspend pudding. Cover with tight-fitting lid; boil 3 hours, adding boiling water as necessary to maintain water level.

6 Untie pudding from handles; place wooden spoon through string loops. Do not put pudding on bench; suspend from spoon by placing over rungs of upturned stool or wedging handle in a drawer. Twist ends of cloth around string to avoid them touching pudding; hang pudding for 10 minutes.

7 Place pudding on board; cut string, carefully peel back cloth. Turn pudding onto a plate; carefully peel cloth away completely. Stand at least 20 minutes or until skin darkens and pudding becomes firm. Dust with icing (confectioner's) sugar, if you like.

NUTRITIONAL COUNT PER SERVING 19.2g total fat (9.3g saturated fat); 1601kJ (383 cal); 62.3g carbohydrate; 7.2g protein; 4.4g fibre

TIPS You need a 60cm (24-inch) square of unbleached calico for the pudding cloth. If the calico has not been used before, soak it in cold water overnight; the next day, boil it for 20 minutes then rinse in cold water.

We used Grand Marnier in this recipe but you could use any citrus-flavoured liqueur you like.

This recipe will make two smaller puddings; use two 40cm (16-inch) squares of calico to make the smaller puddings. Boil puddings in separate boilers for 2 hours. If you only have one boiler, the pudding mixture will stand at room temperature while you cook the first one.

RICH FRUIT CAKES

PREP + COOK TIME 2 HOURS 20 MINUTES (+ STANDING & COOLING)   MAKES 6

3 cups (500g) sultanas

1½ cups (225g) raisins, chopped coarsely

¾ cup (120g) dried currants

⅔ cup (110g) mixed peel

1 cup (200g) glacé cherries, halved

2 tablespoons orange marmalade

¾ cup (180ml) dark rum

250g (8 ounces) butter, softened

1 teaspoon finely grated orange rind

1 teaspoon finely grated lemon rind

1 cup (220g) firmly packed light brown sugar

4 eggs

2 cups (300g) plain (all-purpose) flour

½ teaspoon bicarbonate of soda (baking soda)

2 teaspoons mixed spice

2 tablespoons orange marmalade, extra, warmed, strained

400g (12½ ounces) ready-made white icing

1 Combine fruit, marmalade and ½ cup of the rum in large bowl; cover, stand at room temperature overnight.

2 Preheat oven to 150°C/300°F. Line six deep 10cm (4-inch) round cake pans with three thicknesses of baking paper, extending paper 5cm (2 inches) above sides.

3 Beat butter, rinds and sugar in small bowl with electric mixer until combined; beat in eggs, one at a time.

4 Mix butter mixture into fruit mixture; stir in sifted dry ingredients. Spread mixture evenly into pans; bake about 1½ hours. Brush hot cakes with remaining rum; cover with foil, cool in pans overnight.

5 Brush tops of cakes with extra marmalade. Roll out icing until 8mm (½-inch) thick. Cut out 6 x 10cm (4-inch) flower shapes from icing; place one shape on top of each cake, smooth surface.

NUTRITIONAL COUNT PER CAKE 39.1g total fat (23.8g saturated fat); 6521kJ (1560 cal); 277.7g carbohydrate; 14.9g protein; 9.4g fibre

TIPS Cake mixture can be baked in these well-buttered pans:

12-hole (¾-cup/180ml) texas muffin pan: bake 1¼ hours

14 holes (¾-cup/180ml) petite loaf pan: bake 1 hour

20 holes (½-cup/125ml) oval friand pan: bake 50 minutes

This recipe is the famous, delicious Australian Women's Weekly fruit cake; it keeps and cuts superbly.

WHITE CHRISTMAS CAKE

PREP + COOK TIME 3 HOURS (+ STANDING & COOLING) SERVES 20

½ cup (115g) coarsely chopped glacé pineapple

¾ cup (150g) halved red and green glacé cherries

½ cup (115g) coarsely chopped glacé ginger

¼ cup (60g) coarsely chopped glacé figs

¼ cup (60g) coarsely chopped glacé apricots

⅓ cup (55g) mixed peel

1 cup (110g) coarsely chopped walnuts

1 tablespoon orange marmalade

2 teaspoons finely grated lemon rind

1 tablespoon honey

¼ cup (60ml) sweet sherry

1 teaspoon vanilla extract

250g (8 ounces) butter, softened

1 cup (220g) caster (superfine) sugar

4 eggs

2¼ cups (335g) plain (all-purpose) flour

FLUFFY FROSTING

1 cup (220g) caster (superfine) sugar

⅓ cup (80ml) water

2 egg whites

1 Combine fruit, nuts, marmalade, rind, honey, sherry and extract in large bowl. Cover; stand at room temperature overnight.

2 Line deep 22cm (9-inch) round cake pan with two layers baking paper, bringing paper 5cm (2 inches) above side of pan.

3 Preheat oven to 150°C/300°F.

4 Beat butter until smooth; add sugar, beat until combined. Beat in eggs, one at a time. Mix butter mixture into fruit mixture; stir in sifted flour. Spread mixture into pan.

5 Bake cake about 2½ hours. Cover cake with foil; cool cake in pan overnight.

6 Make fluffy frosting. Spread frosting all over cake. Decorate with Christmas ornaments before frosting sets.

FLUFFY FROSTING Stir sugar and the water in small saucepan, over heat, without boiling, until sugar dissolves. Boil, uncovered, without stirring, about 5 minutes or until syrup reaches 116°C/240°F on a candy thermometer. Syrup should be thick but not coloured. Remove syrup from heat, allow bubbles to subside. Beat egg whites in small bowl with electric mixer until soft peaks form. With motor operating, add hot syrup in a thin steady stream; beat on high speed about 10 minutes or until mixture is thick.

NUTRITIONAL COUNT PER SERVING 15.3g total fat (7.3g saturated fat); 1204kJ (288 cal); 55g carbohydrate; 4.5g protein; 1.2g fibre

TIP You can also make this cake in a deep 20cm (8-inch) square cake pan.

MINI BOILED CHRISTMAS PUDDINGS

PREP + COOK TIME 5 HOURS (+ STANDING) MAKES 6

1 cup (150g) raisins, chopped coarsely

1 cup (160g) sultanas

1 cup (150g) finely chopped seeded dried dates

½ cup (95g) finely chopped seeded prunes

½ cup (85g) mixed peel

½ cup (125g) finely chopped glacé apricots

1 teaspoon finely grated lemon rind

2 tablespoons lemon juice

2 tablespoons apricot jam

2 tablespoons brandy

250g (8 ounces) butter, softened

2 cups (440g) firmly packed light brown sugar

5 eggs

1¼ cups (185g) plain (all-purpose) flour

½ teaspoon each ground nutmeg and
    mixed spice

4 cups (280g) stale breadcrumbs

1 cup (150g) plain (all-purpose) flour, extra

6 x 30cm (12-inch) squares unbleached calico
    (see tips)

1 Combine fruit, rind, juice, jam and brandy in large bowl. Cover; stand in cool, dark place for one week, stirring every day.

2 Beat butter and sugar in small bowl with electric mixer until combined. Beat in eggs, one at a time. Mix butter mixture into fruit mixture. Stir in sifted dry ingredients and breadcrumbs.

3 Fill boiler three-quarters full of hot water, cover with tight lid; bring to the boil. Have ready 1-metre (1-yard) length of kitchen string. Wearing thick rubber gloves, dip pudding cloths, one at a time, into boiling water; boil 1 minute then remove, squeeze excess water from cloth. Spread hot cloths on bench; rub 2 tablespoons of the extra flour into centre of each cloth to cover an area about 18cm (7¼-inch) in diameter, leaving flour a little thicker in centre of cloth where "skin" on the pudding needs to be thickest.

4 Divide pudding mixture equally among cloths; placing in centre of each cloth. Gather cloths around mixture, avoiding any deep pleats; pat into round shapes. Tie cloths tightly with string as close to mixture as possible. Tie loops in string. Lower three puddings into the boiling water. Cover, boil 2 hours, replenishing with boiling water as necessary to maintain water level.

5 Lift puddings from water using wooden spoons through string loops. Do not put puddings on bench; suspend from spoon by placing over rungs of upturned stool or wedging the spoon in a drawer. Twist ends of cloth around string to avoid them touching puddings; hang 10 minutes. Repeat with remaining puddings.

6 Place puddings on board; cut string, carefully peel back cloth. Turn puddings onto plates then carefully peel cloth away completely. Stand at least 20 minutes or until skin darkens and pudding becomes firm.

NUTRITIONAL COUNT PER PUDDING 41.4g total fat (24.4g saturated fat); 5848kJ (1399 cal); 233.4g carbohydrate; 21g protein; 10.7g fibre

TIPS You need six 30cm (12-inch) squares of unbleached calico for each pudding cloth. If the calico has not been used before, soak it in cold water overnight; the next day, boil it for 20 minutes then rinse in cold water.

Puddings can be cooked in two boilers or in batches; the mixture will keep at room temperature for several hours.

Top puddings with a slice of glacé orange, if you like. It is available from gourmet and health-food stores. This recipe makes six generous single servings.

ECCLES MINCE PIES

PREP + COOK TIME **1 HOUR (+ REFRIGERATION)** MAKES 63

7 sheets puff pastry
1 egg white, beaten lightly
1½ tablespoons white (granulated) sugar
FRUIT MINCE
1 cup (150g) raisins
1 cup (160g) dried currants
1 cup (160g) sultanas
1 slice (35g) dried pineapple
2 tablespoons glacé cherries
1 large apple (200g), peeled, grated
¼ cup (40g) blanched almonds
½ cup (110g) lightly packed light brown sugar
50g (1½ ounces) butter, melted
1 tablespoon finely grated orange rind
¼ cup (60ml) orange juice
¼ cup (60ml) brandy
½ teaspoon mixed spice

1 Make fruit mince.
2 Preheat oven to 200°C/400°F. Line oven trays with baking paper.
3 Cut each pastry sheet into nine squares. Top each square with heaped teaspoons of fruit mince; brush pastry edges with egg white. Gather sides of pastry together to enclose filling; turn pies upside down onto trays. Gently flatten pies; cut two slits in top of pies. Brush pies with egg white; sprinkle with sugar.
4 Bake pies about 15 minutes or until golden brown.
FRUIT MINCE Process dried fruit and nuts until coarsely chopped. Transfer mixture to large bowl; stir in remaining ingredients. Cover; refrigerate at least 2 days, stirring every day.
NUTRITIONAL COUNT PER PIE 5.3g total fat (0.8g saturated fat); 485kJ (116 cal); 15.1g carbohydrate; 1.5g protein; 0.8g fibre
TIPS Fruit mince will keep for at least a year in an airtight container in the fridge. The flavours will intensify the longer it is left before using. This recipe makes 3½ cups. You can also use ready-made fruit mince if you're running out of time. You can fill and shape the pies, and freeze in an airtight container for up to 2 months. Brush frozen pies with egg white, sprinkle with sugar and bake about 20 minutes.

Make your 'BIG SISTER' rich fruit cake into a wonderful

Christmas cake

You can't improve on the rich, fruity goodness of 'Big Sister'! Every bite has the flavour of juicy, red cherries, sun-ripe raisins and currants, tender citrus peels and fine old brandy and rum. But you, yourself, can turn it into the finest Christmas cake ever iced, with the wonderful, up-to-date yet simple icing that has been made specially for 'Big Sister' by one of the foremost cooking authorities in this country.

GET YOUR 'BIG SISTER' FRUIT CAKE

FROM YOUR GROCER TODAY . . .

AND DON'T FORGET

'BIG SISTER' PLUM PUDDING

Exclusive 'BIG SISTER'

Christmas Icing

by *Janet Blair*

3 lbs. pure icing sugar	½ teaspoon lemon juice
3 ozs. liquid glucose	½ teaspoon vanilla
2 egg whites	red and green food colouring

Reserve half of one egg white. Drop balance (unbeaten) into middle of sifted icing sugar in bowl. Add melted glucose, lemon juice and vanilla. Work sugar in from the sides until a smooth, stiff paste is formed. Lift on to board dusted with sifted icing sugar. Knead like pastry until icing has absorbed sufficient sugar to hold its shape. Cut off a small portion for decoration. Roll balance to a 12" square, barely ½" thick with rolling pin coated with icing sugar. Brush cake with remaining egg white, lift icing on to cake. Mould and smooth over top and sides of cake with hands coated with icing sugar. Trim excess icing from bottom edges with sharp knife. Add dabs of green colouring to threequarters of portion saved for decoration, knead until evenly coloured. Roll to ¼" thickness. Cut out Christmas trees as illustrated, using paper pattern and small sharp-pointed knife. Moisten trees underneath with egg white, press lightly on to cake. Colour balance of icing red and cut tubs for trees. Apply to cake in same way.

BUTTER ICING FOR PIPING

3 tablespoons soft butter icing made by creaming 1 level tablespoon butter with 1 cup sifted icing sugar and 1 or 2 teaspoons orange juice or sherry. Colour half the butter icing red, balance green. Use to pipe "Merry Christmas", edge decoration and lattice on sides.

Allow cake to stand for 24 hours before cutting.

Big Sister
RICH FRUIT CAKE

F LILLIS & CO. LIMITED, SYDNEY—MAKERS OF FRUIT MIX, COCKTAIL CHERRIES, CH

THE AUSTRALIAN WOMEN'S WEEKLY—No

CHRISTMAS PUDDING COOKIES

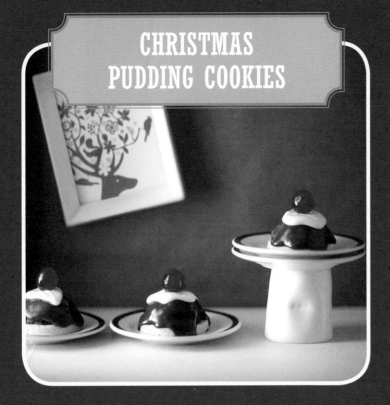

PREP + COOK TIME 45 MINUTES
(+ REFRIGERATION & COOLING) MAKES 30

1²⁄₃ cups (250g) plain (all-purpose) flour
⅓ cup (40g) ground almonds
⅓ cup (75g) caster (superfine) sugar • 1 teaspoon mixed spice
1 teaspoon vanilla extract • 125g (8 ounces) cold butter, chopped
2 tablespoons water • 700g (1½ pounds) rich dark fruit cake
⅓ cup (80ml) brandy • 1 egg white
400g (12½ ounces) dark eating (semi-sweet) chocolate, melted
½ cup (75g) white chocolate melts, melted • 30 red glacé cherries

1 Process flour, ground almonds, sugar, spice, extract and butter until crumbly. Add the water, process until ingredients come together. Knead dough on floured surface until smooth; roll dough between sheets of baking paper until 5mm (¼-inch) thick. Cover; refrigerate 30 minutes.
2 Preheat oven to 180°C/350°F. Grease oven trays; line with baking paper.
3 Cut 30 x 5.5cm (2¼-inch) rounds from dough. Place about 2.5cm (1 inch) apart on oven trays. Bake about 10 minutes.
4 Meanwhile, crumble fruit cake into medium bowl; add brandy. Press mixture firmly into round metal tablespoon measures.
5 Brush partially baked cookies with egg white, top with fruit cake domes; bake 5 minutes. Cool on wire racks. Place wire racks over oven tray, coat cookies with dark chocolate; set at room temperature. Spoon white chocolate over cookies; top with cherries, stand until set.
NUTRITIONAL COUNT PER COOKIE 11.8g total fat (7.5g saturated fat); 1053kJ (252 cal); 34.7g carbohydrate; 3.3g protein; 1.9g fibre

STICKY DATE COOKIES

PREP + COOK TIME 35 MINUTES
(+ REFRIGERATION & COOLING) MAKES 30

1 cup (140g) coarsely chopped seeded dried dates
2 tablespoons golden syrup or treacle • 2 tablespoons water
¼ teaspoon bicarbonate of soda (baking soda)
1 teaspoon finely grated orange rind
1¾ cups (255g) plain (all-purpose) flour
¾ cup (165g) caster (superfine) sugar
100g (3 ounces) butter, chopped coarsely
1 egg • ¼ cup (40g) icing (confectioners') sugar

1 Preheat oven to 180°C/350°F. Grease oven trays; line with baking paper.
2 Bring dates, syrup and the water to the boil in small saucepan. Remove from heat, stir in soda and rind; stand 5 minutes. Process date mixture until almost smooth; cool.
3 Add flour, caster sugar, butter and egg to processor. Process until ingredients come together. Refrigerate mixture 30 minutes.
4 Roll heaped teaspoons of mixture into balls; flatten slightly. Place about 2.5cm (1 inch) apart on oven trays.
5 Bake cookies about 15 minutes. Cool on trays; toss in sifted icing sugar.
NUTRITIONAL COUNT PER COOKIE 2.9g total fat (1.8g saturated fat); 334kJ (80 cal); 17.5g carbohydrate; 1.3g protein; 0.8g fibre

· GLOSSARY ·

ALLSPICE also called pimento or jamaican pepper; tastes like a combination of nutmeg, cumin, clove and cinnamon. Available whole or ground.

ALMONDS

blanched brown skins removed.

flaked paper-thin slices.

ground also called almond meal; nuts are powdered to a coarse flour-like texture.

slivered small pieces cut lengthways.

ANCHOVY FILLETS small oily fish fillets; preserved and packed in oil or salt in small cans or jars; strong in flavour. Fresh anchovies are much milder in flavour.

ARROWROOT a starch made from the rhizome of a Central American plant, used mostly as a thickening agent.

BACON also known as bacon slices.

BAKING PAPER also called parchment paper or baking parchment – is a silicone-coated paper that is primarily used for lining baking pans and oven trays so cakes and biscuits won't stick, making removal easy.

BAKING POWDER a raising agent consisting mainly of two parts cream of tartar to one part bicarbonate of soda.

BAY LEAVES aromatic leaves from the bay tree available fresh or dried; adds a peppery flavour.

BEANS

green also called french or string beans (although the tough string they once had has been bred out of them), this long thin fresh bean is consumed in its entirety once cooked.

white a generic term we use for canned or dried cannellini, haricot, navy or great northern beans.

BEEF

corned also called corned silverside; little fat, cut from the upper leg and cured. Sold cryovac-packed in brine.

eye fillet tenderloin, fillet; fine texture, most expensive and extremely tender.

BEETROOT (BEETS) a firm, round root vegetable.

BICARBONATE OF SODA also known as baking soda.

BREAD

brioche French in origin; a rich, yeast-leavened, cake-like bread made with butter and eggs. Available from cake or specialty bread shops.

ciabatta in Italian, the word means slipper, the traditional shape of this popular crisp-crusted, open-textured white sourdough bread. A good bread to use for bruschetta.

turkish also known as pide. Sold in long (about 45cm) flat loaves as well as individual rounds; made from wheat flour and sprinkled with black onion seeds.

BREADCRUMBS

packaged prepared fine-textured but crunchy white breadcrumbs; good for coating foods that are to be fried.

stale crumbs made by grating, blending or processing one- or two- day-old bread.

BUCKWHEAT a herb in the same plant family as rhubarb; not a cereal so it is gluten-free. Available as flour; ground (cracked) into coarse, medium or fine granules (kasha) and used similarly to polenta; or groats, the whole kernel sold roasted as a cereal product.

BUTTER we use salted butter unless stated otherwise; 125g is equal to 1 stick (4 ounces).

BUTTERMILK originally the term given to the slightly sour liquid left after butter was churned from cream, today it is made from no-fat or low-fat milk to which specific bacterial cultures have been added. Despite its name, it is low in fat.

CAPERBERRIES olive-sized fruit formed after the buds of the caper bush have flowered; they are usually sold pickled in a vinegar brine with stalks intact.

CAPERS the grey-green buds of a warm climate shrub, sold either dried and salted or pickled in a vinegar brine; tiny young ones, called baby capers, are available in brine or dried in salt.

CAPSICUM (BELL PEPPER) also called pepper or bell pepper; comes in different shapes, sizes and colours. Discard seeds and membranes before use.

CARAWAY SEEDS the small, half-moon-shaped dried seed from a member of the parsley family; adds a sharp anise flavour when used in both sweet and savoury dishes.

CARDAMOM a spice native to India and used extensively in its cuisine; can be purchased in pod, seed or ground form.

CHEESE

blue mould-treated cheeses mottled with blue veining.

bocconcini from the diminutive of "boccone", meaning mouthful in Italian; walnut-sized, baby mozzarella. A delicate, semi-soft, white cheese traditionally made from buffalo milk. Sold fresh, it spoils rapidly so will only keep, refrigerated in brine, 1 or 2 days at the most.

cream cheese commonly called philadelphia or philly; a soft cow's-milk cheese, its fat content ranges from 14 to 33%.

fetta Greek in origin; a crumbly textured goat- or sheep-milk cheese with a sharp, salty taste. Ripened and stored in salted whey.

goat's made from goat's milk, has an earthy, strong taste. Available in soft, crumbly and firm textures, in various shapes and sizes, and sometimes rolled in ash or herbs.

haloumi a Greek Cypriot cheese with a semi-firm, spongy texture and very salty sweet flavour. Ripened and stored in salted whey; best grilled or fried, and holds its shape well on being heated. Eat while still warm as it becomes tough and rubbery on cooling.

mascarpone an Italian fresh cultured-cream product made in much the same way as yogurt. Whiteish to creamy yellow in colour, with a soft, creamy buttery-rich, luscious texture.

mozzarella soft, spun-curd cheese; originated in southern Italy. Traditionally made from water-buffalo milk, but now generally made from cow's milk. A popular pizza cheese because of its low melting point and elasticity when heated.

parmesan also called parmigiano; is a hard, grainy cow's-milk cheese originating in Italy. Reggiano is the best variety.

pizza cheese a commercial blend of varying proportions of processed grated mozzarella, cheddar and parmesan.

ricotta a soft, sweet, moist, white cow's-milk cheese with a low fat content (8.5%) and a slightly grainy texture. The name roughly translates as "cooked again" and refers to ricotta's manufacture from a whey that is itself a by-product of other cheese making.

CHERVIL also called cicily; mildly fennel-flavoured member of the parsley family with curly dark-green leaves. Available both fresh and dried but, like all herbs, is best used fresh; like coriander and parsley.

CHICKEN

breast fillet breast halved, skinned and boned.

drumette small fleshy part of the wing between shoulder and elbow, trimmed to resemble a drumstick.

drumstick leg with skin and bone intact.

small chicken also called spatchcock or poussin; no more than 6 weeks old, weighing a maximum of 500g (1 pound). Also a cooking term to describe splitting a small chicken open, flattening then grilling.

tenderloin thin strip of meat lying just under the breast; good for stir-frying.

thigh skin and bone intact.

thigh cutlet thigh with skin and centre bone intact; sometimes found skinned with bone intact.

thigh fillet thigh with skin and centre bone removed.

CHICKPEAS (GARBANZO BEANS) also called hummus or channa; an irregularly round, sandy-coloured legume used in Mediterranean, Indian and Hispanic cooking. Firm texture even after cooking, a floury mouth-feel and robust nutty flavour; available canned or dried (reconstitute for several hours in cold water before use).

CHILLI use rubber gloves when handling fresh chillies as they can burn your skin. We use unseeded chillies because the seeds contain the heat; use fewer chillies rather than seed the lot.

cayenne pepper a thin-fleshed, long, extremely hot dried red chilli, usually purchased ground.

chipotle pronounced cheh-pot-lay. Dried and smoked jalapeño chilli. Has a deep, intensely smoky flavour, the chipotle is dark brown in colour and wrinkled in appearance.
green any unripened chilli; also some particular varieties that are ripe when green, such as jalapeño, habanero, poblano or serrano.
jalapeño pronounced hah-lah-pen-yo. Fairly hot, medium-sized, plump, dark green chilli; available pickled, sold canned or bottled, and fresh.
long red available both fresh and dried; a generic term used for any moderately hot, long, thin chilli (about 6cm to 8cm long).
red thai (serrano) also called scuds or bird's eye chillies; tiny, very hot and bright red.

CHIVES related to the onion and leek; has a subtle onion flavour. Used more for flavour than as an ingredient; chopped finely, they're good in sauces, dressings, omelettes or as a garnish.

CHOCOLATE
dark eating (semi-sweet) also known as luxury chocolate; made of a high percentage of cocoa liquor and cocoa butter, and little added sugar. Unless stated otherwise, we use dark eating chocolate in this book as it's ideal for use in desserts and cakes.
melts small discs of compounded milk, white or dark chocolate ideal for melting and moulding.
milk most popular eating chocolate, mild and very sweet; similar in make-up to dark with the difference being the addition of milk solids.
white eating contains no cocoa solids but derives its sweet flavour from cocoa butter. Very sensitive to heat.

CHORIZO sausage of Spanish origin, made of coarsely ground pork and highly seasoned with garlic and chilli. They are deeply smoked, very spicy and dry-cured so that they do not need cooking.

CINNAMON available in pieces (called sticks or quills) and ground into powder; one of the world's most common spices.

CLOVES dried flower buds of a tropical tree; available whole or ground. Has a strong scent and taste so use sparingly.

COCOA POWDER also called unsweetened cocoa; cocoa beans (cacao seeds) that have been fermented, roasted, shelled, ground into powder then cleared of most of the fat content.

COCONUT
desiccated concentrated, dried, unsweetened and finely shredded coconut flesh.
flaked dried flaked coconut flesh.
shredded unsweetened thin strips of dried coconut flesh.

CORIANDER (CILANTRO) also called pak chee or chinese parsley; bright-green-leafed herb with both pungent aroma and taste. Both the stems and roots of coriander are used in Thai cooking: wash well before chopping. Coriander seeds are dried and sold either whole or ground, and neither form tastes remotely like the fresh leaf.

CORNFLOUR (CORNSTARCH) available made from corn or wheat; used as a thickening agent in cooking.

CORNICHONS French for gherkin, a very small variety of cucumber. Pickled, they are a traditional accompaniment to pâté; the Swiss always serve them with fondue (or raclette).

COUSCOUS a fine, grain-like cereal product made from semolina; from the countries of North Africa. A semolina flour and water dough is sieved then dehydrated to produce minuscule even-sized pellets of couscous; it is rehydrated by steaming or with the addition of a warm liquid and swells to three or four times its original size; eaten like rice with a tagine, as a side dish or salad ingredient.

CRANBERRIES available dried and frozen; have a rich, astringent flavour and can be used in cooking sweet and savoury dishes. The dried version can usually be substituted for or with other dried fruit.

CREAM
pouring also called fresh cream or pure cream. It has no additives, unlike thickened cream. Minimum fat content 35%.
thickened (heavy) a whipping cream containing a thickener. Minimum fat content 35%.

CREAM OF TARTAR the acid ingredient in baking powder; added to confectionery mixtures to help prevent sugar from crystallising. Keeps frostings creamy and improves volume when beating egg whites.

CREME FRAICHE a mature, naturally fermented cream with a velvety texture and slightly tangy, nutty flavour; minimum fat content 35%. A French variation of sour cream, it boils without curdling and can be used in sweet and savoury dishes.

CUCUMBER, LEBANESE short, slender and thin-skinned cucumber. Probably the most popular variety because of its tender, edible skin, tiny, yielding seeds, and sweet, fresh and flavoursome taste.

CUMIN also called zeera or comino; resembling caraway in size, cumin is the dried seed of a plant related to the parsley family. Its spicy, almost curry-like flavour is essential to the traditional foods of Mexico, India, North Africa and the Middle East. Available dried as seeds or ground.

CUSTARD POWDER instant mixture used to make pouring custard; it is similar to North American instant pudding mixes.

DUKKAH an Egyptian specialty spice mixture made up of roasted nuts, seeds and an array of aromatic spices.

EGGPLANT also called aubergine. Ranging in size from tiny to very large and in colour from pale green to deep purple. Can also be purchased char-grilled, packed in oil, in jars.

EGGS we use large chicken eggs weighing an average of 60g unless stated otherwise. If a recipe calls for raw or barely cooked eggs, exercise caution if there is a salmonella problem in your area, particularly in food eaten by children and pregnant women.

ESSENCE either a distilled concentration of a food quality or an artificial creation of it. Coconut and almond essences are synthetically produced substances used in small amounts to impart their respective flavours to foods. Essences keep indefinitely if stored in a cool dark place.

FENNEL also called finocchio or anise; a crunchy green vegetable slightly resembling celery that's eaten raw in salads; fried as an accompaniment; or used as an ingredient in soups and sauces. Also the name given to the dried seeds of the plant which have a stronger licorice flavour.

FISH SAUCE called naam pla if Thai-made, nuoc naam if Vietnamese; the two are almost identical. Made from pulverised salted fermented fish (most often anchovies); has a pungent smell and strong taste. Available in varying degrees of intensity, use according to your taste.

FLOUR

buckwheat see buckwheat

chickpea (besan) also known as gram; made from ground chickpeas so is gluten-free and high in protein. Used in Indian cooking to make dumplings, noodles and chapati; for a batter coating for deep-frying; and as a sauce thickener.

plain (all-purpose) unbleached wheat flour; is the best for baking as the gluten content ensures a strong dough for a light result.

self-raising (self-rising) plain flour sifted with added baking powder; make at home in the proportion of 1 cup flour to 2 teaspoons baking powder.

GELATINE we use dried (powdered) gelatine in this book; it's also available in sheet form known as leaf gelatine. Three teaspoons of dried gelatine (8g or one sachet) is about the same as four gelatine leaves. The two types are interchangable but leaf gelatine gives a much clearer mixture than dried gelatine.

GINGER

fresh also called green or root ginger; the thick gnarled root of a tropical plant. Can be kept, peeled, covered with dry sherry in a jar and refrigerated, or frozen in an airtight container.

glacé fresh ginger root preserved in sugar syrup; crystallised ginger can be used if rinsed with warm water and dried before using.

ground also called powdered ginger; used as a flavouring in baking but cannot be substituted for fresh ginger.

GLACE CHERRIES also called candied cherries; boiled in a heavy sugar syrup and then dried.

GLACE FRUIT fruit, such as peaches, pineapple and oranges, cooked in a heavy sugar syrup then dried.

GLUCOSE SYRUP also known as liquid glucose, made from wheat starch. Available at most supermarkets.

GOLDEN SYRUP a by-product of refined sugarcane; pure maple syrup or honey can be substituted. Treacle is similar however, it is more viscous and has a stronger flavour and aroma – golden syrup has been refined further and contains fewer impurities, so is lighter in colour and more fluid.

HORSERADISH purchased in bottles at the supermarket in two forms: horseradish cream and prepared horseradish. These cannot be substituted one for the other in cooking but both can be used as table condiments.

cream commercially prepared creamy paste consisiting of grated horseradish, vinegar, oil and sugar.

prepared preserved grated horseradish.

KAFFIR LIME LEAVES also known as bai magrood and looks like two glossy dark green leaves joined end to end, forming a rounded hourglass shape. Used fresh or dried in many South-East Asian dishes, they are used like bay leaves or curry leaves. Sold fresh, dried or frozen, the dried leaves are less potent so double the number if using them as a substitute for fresh; a strip of fresh lime peel may be substituted for each kaffir lime leaf.

KALONJI also called nigella seeds or black onion seeds. Tiny, angular seeds, black on the outside and creamy within, with a sharp nutty flavour that is enhanced by frying briefly in a dry hot pan before use. Can be found in most Middle-Eastern and Asian food shops. Sometimes erroneously called black cumin seeds.

KECAP MANIS a dark, thick, sweet soy sauce used in most South-East Asian cuisines.

KITCHEN STRING made of a natural product, so it neither affects the flavour of the food it's tied around nor melts when heated.

KUMARA the Polynesian name of an orange-fleshed sweet potato often confused with yam; good baked, boiled, mashed or fried similarly to other potatoes.

LAMB

backstrap also known as eye of loin; the larger fillet from a row of loin chops or cutlets. Tender, best cooked rapidly: barbecued or pan-fried.

cutlet small, tender rib chop; sometimes sold french-trimmed, with all the fat and gristle at the narrow end of the bone removed.

shank forequarter leg; sometimes sold as drumsticks or frenched shanks if the gristle and narrow end of the bone are discarded and the remaining meat trimmed.

LIMONCELLO LIQUEUR Italian lemon-flavoured liqueur; originally made from the juice and peel of lemons grown along the Amalfi coast.

MAPLE-FLAVOURED SYRUP is made from sugar cane and is also known as golden or pancake syrup. It is not a substitute for pure maple syrup.

MAPLE SYRUP (PURE) distilled from the sap of sugar maple trees. Maple-flavoured syrup or pancake syrup is not an adequate substitute for the real thing.

MARZIPAN made from ground almonds, sugar and glucose. Similar to almond paste, however, is not as strong in flavour, has a finer consistency and is more pliable. Cheaper brands often use ground apricot kernels and sugar.

MILK we use full-cream homogenised milk unless stated.

MIXED PEEL candied citrus peel.

MIXED SPICE a classic spice mixture generally containing caraway, allspice, coriander, cumin, nutmeg and ginger, although cinnamon and other spices can be added. It is used with fruit and in cakes.

MORELLO SOUR CHERRIES bitter cherries available bottled in syrup. Used in baking and savoury dishes and a good match for game.

MUSHROOMS

button small, cultivated white mushrooms with a mild flavour. When a recipe in this book calls for an unspecified mushroom, use button.

enoki cultivated mushrooms also called enokitake; are tiny long-stemmed, pale mushrooms that grow and are sold in clusters, and can be used that way or separated by slicing off the base. Have a mild fruity flavour and slightly crisp texture.

oyster also known as abalone; grey-white mushrooms shaped like a fan. Prized for their smooth texture and subtle, oyster-like flavour.

shiitake, fresh also called chinese black, forest or golden oak mushrooms. Although cultivated, they have the earthiness and taste of wild mushrooms. They are large and meaty.

swiss brown also called roman or cremini. Light to dark brown mushrooms with full-bodied flavour; suited for use in casseroles or being stuffed and baked.

MUSTARD

american-style bright yellow in colour, a sweet mustard containing mustard seeds, sugar, salt, spices and garlic. Serve with hot dogs and hamburgers.

dijon also called french. Pale brown, creamy, distinctively flavoured, fairly mild french mustard.

wholegrain also called seeded. A French-style coarse-grain mustard made from crushed mustard seeds and dijon-style french mustard. Works well with cold meats and sausages.

NORI a type of dried seaweed used in Japanese cooking as a garnish, flavouring or for sushi. Sold in thin sheets, plain or toasted (yaki-nori).

NUTMEG a strong and pungent spice ground from the dried nut of an evergreen tree native to Indonesia. Usually found ground but the flavour is more intense from a whole nut, so it's best to grate your own. Available from spice shops.

OIL

cooking spray we use a cholesterol-free cooking spray made from canola oil.

olive made from ripened olives. Extra virgin and virgin are the first and second press, respectively, of the olives and are therefore considered the best; the "extra light" or "light" name on other types refers to taste not fat levels.

peanut pressed from ground peanuts; the most commonly used oil in Asian cooking because of its high smoke point (capacity to handle high heat without burning).

sesame made from roasted, crushed, white sesame seeds; a flavouring rather than a cooking medium.

vegetable any oils from plant rather than animal fats.

ONION

brown strongly-flavoured onions with a brown skin and creamy flesh; the most commonly used onion in cooking.

green (scallions) also called (incorrectly) shallot; an immature onion picked before the bulb has formed, having a long, bright-green edible stalk.

red also known as spanish, red spanish or bermuda onion; a large, sweet tasting, purple-red onion.

shallots also called french shallots, golden shallots or eschalots. Small and elongated, with a brown-skin, they grow in tight clusters similar to garlic.

spring crisp, narrow green-leafed tops and a round sweet white bulb larger than green onions.

PANCETTA an Italian unsmoked bacon; pork belly is cured in salt and spices then rolled into a sausage shape and dried for several weeks.

PAPRIKA ground dried sweet red capsicum (bell pepper); there are many types available, including hot, sweet, mild and smoked.

PINE NUTS also called pignoli; not a nut but a small, cream-coloured kernel from pine cones. They are best roasted before use to bring out the flavour.

POLENTA also called cornmeal; a flour-like cereal of dried corn (maize). Also the dish made from it.

PORK

cutlets cut from ribs.
fillet skinless, boneless eye-fillet cut from the loin.
minced ground lean pork.
shoulder joint sold with bone in or out.

POTATO

desiree oval, smooth and pink-skinned, waxy yellow flesh; good in salads, boiled and roasted.
kipfler (fingerling) small, finger-shaped, nutty flavour; great baked and in salads.
pontiac large, red skin, deep eyes, white flesh; good grated, boiled and baked.
russet burbank long and oval, rough white skin with shallow eyes, white flesh; good for baking and frying.
sebago white skin, oval; good fried, mashed and baked.

PRESERVED LEMON whole or quartered salted lemons preserved in a mixture of water, lemon juice, or olive oil, and occasionally with spices such as cinnamon, coriander and cloves. Use the rind only and rinse well under cold water before using.

PROSCIUTTO a kind of unsmoked Italian ham; salted, air-cured and aged, it is usually eaten uncooked.

QUAIL small, delicate flavoured, domestically grown game birds ranging in weight from 250g to 300g (8-9½ ounces). Also known as partridge.

QUINCE yellow-skinned fruit with hard texture and astringent, tart taste; eaten cooked or as a preserve. Long, slow cooking makes the flesh a deep rose pink.

RADICCHIO Italian in origin; a member of the chicory family. The dark burgundy leaves and strong, bitter flavour can be cooked or eaten raw in salads.

RHUBARB a plant with long, green-red stalks; becomes sweet and edible when cooked.

RICE

arborio small, round grain rice well-suited to absorb a large amount of liquid; the high level of starch makes it especially suitable for risottos, giving the dish its classic creaminess.
basmati a white, fragrant long-grained rice; the grains fluff up when cooked. Wash several times before cooking.

RISONI small rice-shape pasta; very similar to another small pasta, orzo.

ROCKET (ARUGULA) also rugula and rucola; peppery green leaf eaten raw in salads or used in cooking. Baby rocket leaves are smaller and less peppery.

ROLLED OATS flattened oat grain rolled into flakes and traditionally used for porridge. Instant oats are also available, but use traditional oats for baking.

SEAFOOD

lobster (rock lobster) also called cray, spiny lobster, eastern, southern or western lobster. Substitute with balmain or moreton bay bugs.
prawns (shrimp) varieties include, school, king, royal red, Sydney harbour, tiger. Can be bought uncooked (green) or cooked, with or without shells.
scallops a bivalve mollusc with fluted shell valve; we use scallops that have the coral (roe) attached.
white fish fillets means non-oily fish; includes bream, flathead, whiting, snapper, dhufish, redfish and ling.

SICHUAN PEPPER the peppercorns are reddish-brown in colour, with a strong, pungent aroma and a sharp, tingling and mildly spicy taste. Dry-roast to bring out their full flavour; grind with a mortar and pestle.

SILVER BEET also called swiss chard and incorrectly, spinach; has fleshy stalks and large leaves, both of which can be prepared as for spinach.

SOY SAUCE

dark deep brown, almost black in colour; rich, with a thicker consistency than other types. Pungent but not particularly salty; good for marinating.
japanese an all-purpose low-sodium soy sauce with more wheat content than its Chinese counterparts; fermented in barrels and aged. Possibly the best table soy and the one to choose if you only want one variety.
light fairly thin in consistency and, while paler than the others, the saltiest tasting; used in dishes in which the natural colour of the ingredients is to be maintained. Not to be confused with salt-reduced or low-sodium soy sauces.

SPINACH (english spinach) also incorrectly called silver beet. Its thick, soft oval leaves and green stems are both edible.

STAR ANISE a dried star-shaped pod whose seeds have an astringent aniseed flavour.

SUGAR

brown a soft, finely granulated sugar retaining molasses for its characteristic colour and flavour.

caster (superfine) finely granulated table sugar.

demerara small-grained golden-coloured crystal sugar.

icing (confectioners') also known as powdered sugar; pulverised granulated sugar crushed together with a small amount of cornflour (cornstarch).

palm also called nam tan pip, jaggery, jawa or gula melaka; made from the sap of the sugar palm tree. Light brown to black in colour and usually sold in rock-hard cakes; substitute with brown sugar.

pure icing (confectioners') also known as powdered sugar.

SUMAC a purple-red, astringent spice ground from berries growing on wild Mediterranean shrubs; adds a tart, lemony flavour. Can be found in Middle Eastern food stores.

TARRAGON French tarragon, with its subtle aniseed flavour is one of the herbs that make up the French "fines herbs". Russian and Mexican tarragons are coarser in texture.

THYME a member of the mint family, it has tiny grey-green leaves that give off a pungent minty, light-lemon aroma. Dried thyme comes in both leaf and powder form. Dried thyme should be stored in a cool, dark place for no more than three months. Fresh thyme should be stored in the refrigerator, wrapped in a damp paper towel and placed in a sealed bag for no more than a few days.

TOMATOES

bottled pasta sauce a prepared sauce; a blend of tomatoes, herbs and spices.

paste triple-concentrated tomato puree.

truss small vine-ripened tomatoes with the vine still attached.

TREACLE thick, dark syrup not unlike molasses; a by-product of sugar refining.

TURMERIC also called kamin; a rhizome related to galangal and ginger. Must be grated or pounded to release its acrid aroma and pungent flavour. Known for the golden colour it imparts, fresh turmeric can be substituted with the more commonly found dried powder. Be aware that fresh turmeric stains your hands and plastic utensils (chopping boards, spatulas, the bowl of a food processor).

VANILLA

bean dried, long, thin pod from a tropical golden orchid; the minuscule black seeds inside the bean are used to impart a luscious vanilla flavour in baking and desserts.

Place a whole bean in a jar of sugar to make vanilla sugar; a bean can be used three or four times.

extract made by extracting the flavour from the vanilla bean pod; pods are soaked, usually in alcohol, to capture the authentic flavour.

paste made from vanilla pods and contains real seeds. Is highly concentrated – 1 teaspoon replaces a whole vanilla pod. Found in most supermarkets in the baking section.

VERJUICE an unfermented grape juice with a fresh lemony-vinegar flavour. It's available from most supermarkets, usually in the vinegar section.

VIETNAMESE MINT not a mint at all, but a pungent and peppery narrow-leafed member of the buckwheat family. Not confined to Vietnam, it is also called cambodian mint, pak pai (Thailand), laksa leaf (Indonesia), daun kesom (Singapore) and rau ram in Vietnam.

VINEGAR

balsamic originally from Modena, Italy, there are now many balsamic vinegars on the market. Quality can be determined up to a point by price; use the most expensive sparingly. Aged balsamic is thicker.

cider made from fermented apples.

malt made from fermented malt and beech shavings.

rice wine made from rice wine lees (sediment left after fermentation), salt and alcohol; used in Asian cooking.

WATERCRESS also called winter rocket, is a slightly peppery, dark-green leafy vegetable commercially cultivated but also found growing in the wild. Highly perishable, so must be used as soon as possible after purchase.

WITLOF (BELGIAN ENDIVE) related to and confused with chicory. A versatile vegetable, it tastes as good cooked as it does raw. Grown in darkness like white asparagus to prevent it becoming green.

WOMBOK (NAPA CABBAGE) also called chinese or peking cabbage; elongated in shape with pale green, crinkly leaves, this is the most common cabbage in South-East Asia.

WORCESTERSHIRE SAUCE thin, dark-brown spicy sauce developed by the British when in India; used as a seasoning for meat, gravies and cocktails.

YEAST (dried and fresh) raising agent used in dough making. Granular (7g sachets) and fresh compressed (20g blocks) yeast can almost always be substituted one for the other when yeast is called for.

YOGURT we use plain full-cream yogurt unless stated otherwise.

ZUCCHINI also called courgette.

CONVERSION CHART

MEASURES

One Australian metric measuring cup holds approximately 250ml; one Australian metric tablespoon holds 20ml; one Australian metric teaspoon holds 5ml.

The difference between one country's measuring cups and another's is within a two- or three-teaspoon variance, and will not affect your cooking results. North America, New Zealand and the United Kingdom use a 15ml tablespoon.

All cup and spoon measurements are level. The most accurate way of measuring dry ingredients is to weigh them. When measuring liquids, use a clear glass or plastic jug with the metric markings.

We use large eggs with an average weight of 60g.

DRY MEASURES

METRIC	IMPERIAL
15g	½ oz
30g	1oz
60g	2oz
90g	3oz
125g	4oz (¼ lb)
155g	5oz
185g	6oz
220g	7oz
250g	8oz (½ lb)
280g	9oz
315g	10oz
345g	11oz
375g	12oz (¾ lb)
410g	13oz
440g	14oz
470g	15oz
500g	16oz (1lb)
750g	24oz (1½ lb)

LIQUID MEASURES

METRIC	IMPERIAL
30ml	1 fluid oz
60ml	2 fluid oz
100ml	3 fluid oz
125ml	4 fluid oz
150ml	5 fluid oz
190ml	6 fluid oz
250ml	8 fluid oz
300ml	10 fluid oz
500ml	16 fluid oz
600ml	20 fluid oz
1000ml (1 litre)	1¾ pints

LENGTH MEASURES

METRIC	IMPERIAL
3mm	⅛ in
6mm	¼ in
1cm	½ in
2cm	¾ in
2.5cm	1in
5cm	2in
6cm	2½ in
8cm	3in
10cm	4in
13cm	5in
15cm	6in
18cm	7in
20cm	8in
22cm	9in
25cm	10in
28cm	11in
30cm	12in (1ft)

OVEN TEMPERATURES

The oven temperatures in this book are for conventional ovens; if you have a fan-forced oven, decrease the temperature by 10-20 degrees.

	°C (CELSIUS)	°F (FAHRENHEIT)
Very slow	120	250
Slow	150	300
Moderately slow	160	325
Moderate	180	350
Moderately hot	200	400
Hot	220	425
Very hot	240	475

The imperial measurements used in these recipes are approximate only. Measurements for cake pans are approximate only. Using same-shaped cake pans of a similar size should not affect the outcome of your baking. We measure the inside top of the cake pan to determine sizes.

INDEX

FIRST PUBLISHED IN 2011 BY ACP BOOKS, SYDNEY
REPRINTED IN 2012
ACP BOOKS ARE PUBLISHED BY ACP MAGAZINES LTD
A DIVISION OF NINE ENTERTAINMENT CO.

54 Park St, Sydney; GPO Box 4088, Sydney, NSW 2001.
phone (02) 9282 8618; fax (02) 9126 3702
acpbooks@acpmagazines.com.au; www.acpbooks.com.au

ACP BOOKS

General Manager CHRISTINE WHISTON

Editor-in-Chief SUSAN TOMNAY

Creative Director HIEU CHI NGUYEN

Art Director & Designer HANNAH BLACKMORE

Senior Editor STEPHANIE KISTNER

Food Director PAMELA CLARK

DISTRIBUTED IN THE UNITED KINGDOM BY
Octopus Publishing Group
Endeavour House
189 Shaftesbury Avenue
London WC2H 8JY
United Kingdom
phone (+44) (0) 207 632 5400; fax (+44) (0) 207 632 5405
info@octopus-publishing.co.uk;
www.octopusbooks.co.uk

PRINTED BY C&C Offset Printing, China

International Foreign Language Rights,
Brian Cearnes, ACP Books bcearnes@acpmagazines.com.au

A catalogue record for this book is available from the British Library.
ISBN 978-1-74245-103-9 (hbk.)